Here We Go Round

Quality Circle Time for 3 – 5 year olds

**Jenny Mosley &
Helen Sonnet**

Positive Press

Published by Positive Press Ltd
28A Gloucester Road
Trowbridge
Wiltshire BA14 0AA
England

First published 2001
Reprinted 2003, 2007
© 2001 Positive Press Ltd
Text © Jenny Mosley and Helen Sonnet

ISBN 9780953012213

Printed by:
HERON PRESS
Westbury, Wiltshire.

Contents

Introduction 1

How Quality Circle Time Works 3
All you need to know for setting up successful
Quality Circle Time sessions for 3-5 year olds.

Introducing Children to Quality Circle Time 11
Activity plans for five introductory sessions

The Six Areas of Learning
Ten sessions of structured circle activities for each area

    Personal, Social and Emotional Development 17

    Communication, Language and Literacy 37

    Mathematical Development 59

    Knowledge and Understanding of the World 79

    Physical Development 97

    Creative Development 115

Training and Resources 137

Acknowledgements

Tremendous thanks are due to our illustrator, Juliet Doyle, for constantly coming up with a fund of lovely ideas and responding so quickly to our requests. An infant teacher for four years, she recently left the classroom to become a mum. Look out for more of her delightful drawings in future publications.

We also wish to extend our warm thanks to:

Catherine Bryant for taking the lovely cover photograph showing the children at her See-Saw Nursery in Trowbridge.

Pat Glass, nursery practitioner in Frome, for her patience in exploring the ideas during the preparation of this book, and for her helpful advice.

Marion Dowling, early years specialist and former HMI, for taking time in her busy life to read and review the book so positively.

Pat Child, Primary PSHE Co-ordinator (Guernsey), for generously making available her time and expertise to read and update the book in the light of latest developments.

Introduction

This is a very timely book. The Qualifications and Curriculum Authority (QCA) published *Early Learning Goals* in October 1999, followed by *Curriculum Guidance for the Foundation Stage* in May 2000. Early Years practitioners are being urged to reassess whether their ethos and practice are sufficiently enriching to stimulate the emotional, social, intellectual and physical growth of young children.

The period from age three to the end of the reception year is described as a distinct foundation stage. 'Practitioners need to plan learning experiences of the highest quality, considering both children's needs and achievements and the range of learning experiences that will help them make progress. Well-planned play is a key way in which children learn with enjoyment and challenge during the foundation stage' (QCA *Guidance*). We maintain that the majority of the recommended goals can be achieved by adults who are prepared to engage with children in the regular practice of the Quality Circle Time Model. We believe that this model has the potential to act as one of the safest yet most stretching foundation strategies available.

The book has been structured to help teachers realise the aims of the six areas of learning. Initially the Circle Time sessions focus on helping children develop the requisite skills and attitudes; the main body of the Circle Time lesson plans then helps the teacher and children explore each of the six areas. The learning objectives are clearly stated at the beginning of each section and each circle session details the particular learning objectives it is helping children to achieve.

From the outset, though, we would like to say that neither the Early Learning Goals nor Quality Circle Time are new or revolutionary! They represent the wealth of common sense and good practice that already abounds in many pre-school settings. Since the beginning of time young children have gathered together in circles to learn about themselves and others through a rich weave of rhymes, songs and games. Getting into a circle is as natural as pie! All this book does is structure these activities in such a way that the adults and children know what they are achieving by doing them. It makes the implicit explicit. Many of you will look at these activities and recognise yourself and the children in them.

How Quality Circle Time Works

The benefits of Quality Circle Time for children

- The activities outlined in this book are designed to encourage the development of high self-esteem and positive attitudes towards others.

- The activities support the aims stated in *Curriculum Guidance for the Foundation Stage* (QCA).

- The process is democratic and provides opportunities for all children to feel equally valued. Regular opportunities are given for children to affirm themselves and others.

- A safe environment is provided in which the children can try out new roles and activities.

- The children engage in a safe yet exciting listening system.

- Time for sharing, turn-taking, and learning to be part of a group is given 'high profile'.

- All the structures and ideas help children to develop good social skills.

- Most importantly, Quality Circle Time is fun and motivates children to learn through their own discovery and exploration.

Quality Circle Time benefits the teacher by:

- Helping to promote the principles for early years education as stated in *Curriculum Guidance for the Foundation Stage*.

- Providing a sounder knowledge of the children.

- Promoting a greater trust in the children's capabilities.

- Providing opportunities to have fun with the children.

- Helping you develop a more thoughtful approach to the children.

- Creating a forum in which to address problems and other issues.

- Ensuring that an ideal opportunity is created for regular observation and assessment.

Setting up Quality Circle Time

You need to select a suitable area in which to hold Circle Time. This should be carpeted and large enough to seat the children with sufficient space to carry out the activities. Initially, it may be difficult for very young children to sit in a circle and concentrate on the activities. Marking a symbolic place for them with their own cushions, carpet squares or small chairs will help. Also, make sure that you hold your circle in an area which is free from distractions, e.g. boxes of toys, books which are within easy reach of the children.

Timetabling Circle Time

Circle Time should be timetabled at least once a week. Once it is up and running it should last for 15–20 minutes, although you may wish to shorten this to 10 minutes for younger children. Choose a time when both you and the children are fresh. It is important that you come to the circle with a positive attitude, so do not choose a time when you know you may be feeling under pressure or stressed.

Circle size

The circle size will depend on the age and ability of the children. Initially, keep the circle small e.g. around six for the very young child, increasing this number to 10–12 for the older ones. Each circle must have at least one adult helper and they must all follow the same lesson plan and its accompanying script. Once the children become familiar and practised in the Circle Time ground rules and routines, it may be possible to draw all adults and children together in regular 'full class' circles so that they can develop a sense of their wider community.

Use of adult helpers

Ensure that adult helpers sit in the circle, either on the floor or on the same sized chairs as the children. Arrange the helpers so that they sit by the children who are most likely to need their help and encouragement, e.g. the youngest children, those who find it difficult to sit still and join in the activities or any child with additional needs. Use special 'Circle Time' invitations to encourage parents to come along and join in and always make sure that you have sufficient helpers to facilitate the smooth and effective running of Circle Time.

Children with additional needs

One of the main principles of Quality Circle Time is that all children should be equally valued and included in the circle. It is therefore important that any child with additional needs is given the necessary support to enable him to participate in Circle Time. This may mean one to one support from an adult helper. The teacher or helper should be informed before Circle Time of the appropriate support that is needed, especially if the child has an Individual Education Plan citing specific targets. Consideration must also be given to include a child whose development is delayed. The helper may need to simplify an activity in order to make it meaningful for the child.

The ground rules of Quality Circle Time

Establishing the ground rules of Circle Time is essential to ensure its success. Initially, children will need to be reminded at the beginning of each Circle Time to observe these ground rules. Thereafter, an occasional reminder should be sufficient.

♦ We will all use a special signal if we want to talk, e.g. hands up, holding the 'talking object'.

♦ We will all listen to each other. No one is allowed to interrupt when someone else is talking. If an adult needs to interrupt in order to help another child keep to the ground rules, she would say to the child who is speaking:

"I am sorry to interrupt, but I just need to remind _____ ".

♦ We all say good things about each other in the circle. No one must use put-downs including laughing at another individual's contribution.

♦ We all have the right to speak up or not to speak up if we don't want to. Children can say 'pass' if it is a round. They will be given a second opportunity to contribute at the end of the round, when the teacher says:

"Does anyone who said 'pass' want another chance to speak?"

Maintaining positive behaviour in the circle

The most effective way to achieve positive behaviour within the circle is to use a proactive approach. Praising good behaviour and awarding stickers which commend positive behaviour are effective, as is 'adjacent praise', the practice of praising a child who is behaving well and is near the child who is not.

If a child continues to be disruptive, a visual warning can be used. This could be a sad face printed onto a card which is placed beside the child when a circle rule has been broken. It is explained that by breaking the circle rules s/he has made you and the class feel sad – but if the child stops breaking the rules we can turn the card over to a happy face as everybody will feel pleased. If the child does not heed the warning, s/he could be asked to sit outside the circle and watch a one minute sand timer and then be invited back with a smile.

NOTE: It is important to remove the warning card once the child has responded to it.

A talking object

When doing a round we use a Talking Object. The object needs to be small such as a painted wooden egg or small teddy, 'Talking Ted', which can be easily passed from child to child around the circle. Some practitioners use an object that begins with the special sound of the week for the setting, thereby reinforcing other curriculum areas.

Each child has a turn to speak when they hold the talking object. Remember, that a child can elect to 'pass'. When you initially introduce Circle Time to the children, use an adult helper to ensure that the talking object passes smoothly around the circle and is not held for too long by any child.

Maintaining the quality of Circle Time

Circle Time is an ideal system in which to enhance self-esteem, deal with problems and topical issues, impart information, motivate the children and encourage self-discipline. However, if it is to maintain its effectiveness, it must remain a time of quality.

It is important to review the quality of your Circle Time each term to ensure that it has not degenerated into merely a 'show and tell' circle, a games circle or a way of filling in spare time. Always use a lesson plan and be clear about the learning objectives you intend to promote. Ensure that Circle Time does not become boring and repetitive and that practitioners are fully aware of the skills they need to use during Circle Time.

These are:

- ◆ Empathic listening
- ◆ The use of good eye contact
- ◆ The ability to show emotional warmth
- ◆ The ability to recap what children have said and reflect it back
- ◆ The ability to respond proactively to negative behaviour
- ◆ The ability to use effective encouragement

The five skills of Circle Time

The children should be taught the five skills of Circle Time which are:

Looking

Listening

Speaking

Thinking

Concentrating

The following short routine can be practised in a circle as a game. Once you have explained the skills to the children, you can say the words while they perform the actions and vice versa. Remind them at the beginning of each Circle Time of these skills.

"In Circle Time we use our looking skills."	Point to eyes.
"We use our listening skills."	Point to ears.
"We use our speaking skills."	Point to mouths.
"We use our thinking skills."	Place hands on sides of head.
"We use our concentrating skills."	Clasp hands and place in laps and look at facilitator.

How to use the session plans

The first five Circle Time sessions act as an introduction to Circle Time for the children and an opportunity to learn and practise the five skills and are scheduled to last 10–15 minutes.

The subsequent Circle Time activity plans are divided into six sections which correspond to the six learning areas of the Early Learning Goals for the foundation stage curriculum. Each Circle Time session states the learning objectives of the activities included which are based on the Early Learning Goals for that particular learning area. At the beginning of each chapter is a list of all the learning objectives covered in that area.

Each Circle Time session is scheduled to last for about 20 minutes. If you feel that this would be too long for your group you can spread the activities over two circle sessions or just select key activities.

Each session advises you of the resources you will need for the activities and may offer further guidelines to assist you. In a very few of the sessions, some activities take place outside the circle.

The sessions have been divided into three phases:

- **An introductory phase**: this may be used for a warm-up activity or to introduce a topic.

- **A middle phase**: this will be used for activities and discussion.

- **A closing phase**: this may be used to round up and reflect on the previous activities or as a calming period.

In some sessions all three phases will include activities.

Introducing Children to Quality Circle Time

Introductory Session 1

Learning Objectives

To learn and practise the Circle Time skills, to take turns, to work as a group.

Resources

A glove puppet. A large ball. Stickers (see Resources section).

Introductory Phase

Go through the five Circle Time skills with the children. Remember to use stickers and praise to reinforce the desired behaviour:

"Well done _____ for using good looking skills."

Introduce the puppet:

"Hello children, I'd like you to meet _____ (puppet's name). S/he would like to know what your names are."

Ask each child in turn around the circle to say:

"Hello _____ (puppet's name), my name is _____ ."

Middle Phase

Ask the children to sit with legs apart. The children roll the ball to one another after saying:

"Hello _____ (name of receiver)."

The child who receives the ball responds by saying:

"Thank you _____ ."

Closing Phase

Pass a smile around the circle. Begin by smiling at the child on your right. This child passes the smile to the child on his right and so on. Encourage the children to make eye contact when they are passing the smile on.

Introductory Session 2

Learning Objectives

To learn and practise the five Circle Time skills, to take turns, to work as a group.

Resources

A talking object e.g. 'Talking Ted'. A bunch of keys or tambourine.

Introductory Phase.

Go through the five Circle Time skills and remember to reinforce good practice. Pass a smile around the circle.

Middle Phase

Introduce 'Talking Ted'. Explain to the children that when they hold 'Ted' they can talk and no one can interrupt them; they will all have a turn to hold him. Passing 'Ted' around the circle, each child says:

"Hello my name is _____ ."

Closing Phase

End by having the children pass the keys around the circle as quietly as possible.

Introductory Session 3

Learning Objectives

To learn and practise the Circle Time skills, to take turns, to work as a group.

Resources

'Talking Ted'.

Introductory Phase

Go through the five Circle Time skills. Ask the children to hold hands around the circle. Emphasising the need to be gentle, send a hand squeeze around the circle from child to child. Tell the children that they must not send the squeeze on until they have received it. If you think your group will find this activity difficult let the children hold hands around the circle then raise and lower arms together.

Middle Phase

Ask the children to copy you as you mime getting up in the morning, getting dressed, washing, cleaning your teeth and brushing your hair. Talk the children through your actions while you are performing them. Try and make it interesting and fun, e.g.

> "Oh! I've lost a sock."

Pretend to look for it:

> "I've got something sticky in my hair. It's very hard to comb. Ooh! ouch!"

Closing Phase

Using 'Talking Ted', end with a round of:

> "In the morning I _____ _____ _____ ."

Introductory Session 4

Learning Objectives

To practise the Circle Time skills, to take turns, to work as a group.

Resources

A ball.

Introductory Phase

Remind the children of the five skills of Circle Time.

The children sit with legs apart. They roll the ball to each other. Each child who receives the ball says:

"My favourite toy is _____ ."

Once a child has had a turn he closes his legs to indicate that he is no longer able to receive the ball.

Middle Phase

Explain to the children that they must listen very carefully as you are going to clap instructions to them.

One clap means stand.

Two claps mean sit.

Three claps mean jump on the spot.

With younger children practice each instruction in turn until they are able to respond correctly.

Closing Phase

Send a gentle hand squeeze around the circle.

Introductory Session 5

Learning Objectives

To practise the Circle Time skills, to take turns, to work as a group.

Resources

A large 'busy' illustration.

Introductory Phase

Ask the children if they would like to lead the five Circle Time skills.

Say to the children that they must listen very carefully as you are going to clap a rhythm for them to copy. Do this several times starting with a very short and simple rhythm.

Middle Phase

Show them the illustration and ask them to look at it very carefully. Ask them questions about it, such as:

"How many _____ are there?"

"What colour is _____ ?"

"What is _____ doing?"

Tell the children they must put their hands up if they know the answer as you will only choose people who have their hands up and are sitting quietly.

Closing Phase

Pass a squeeze around the circle, first in a clockwise direction then in an anti-clockwise direction. Remind the children that they must wait for the squeeze to reach them before they can pass it on.

The Six Areas of Learning

1. Personal, Social and Emotional Development

'This area of learning is about emotional well-being, knowing who you are and where you fit in and feeling good about yourself. It is also about developing respect for others, social competence and a positive disposition to learn' – QCA Curriculum Guidance

Learning objectives covered in this section are:

♦ Continue to be interested, excited and motivated to learn

♦ Be confident to try new activities, initiate ideas and speak in a familiar group

♦ Maintain attention, concentrate and sit quietly when appropriate

♦ Work as part of a group, taking turns and sharing fairly, understanding that there need to be agreed values and codes of behaviour for groups of people to work together harmoniously

(these four objectives apply to Circle Time in general)

♦ Have a developing awareness of their own needs, views and feelings and be sensitive to the needs, views and feelings of others

♦ Have a developing respect for their own cultures and beliefs and those of other people

♦ Respond to significant experiences, showing a range of feelings when appropriate

♦ Form good relationships with adults and peers

♦ Understand what is right and wrong and why

♦ Consider the consequences of their words and actions for themselves and others

♦ Understand that people have different needs, views, cultures and beliefs, which need to be treated with respect

♦ Understand that they can expect others to treat their needs, views, cultures and beliefs with respect

♦ Dress and undress independently and manage personal hygiene

Feeling Happy

Learning Objectives

To have a developing awareness of their own needs, views and feelings and form good relationships with their peers.

Resources

A talking object.

Introductory Phase

Ask the children to look at you. Make a happy face and ask them to guess how you are feeling. Repeat with a sad face. Ask them to make sad/happy faces.

Middle Phase

Ask the children what sorts of thing make them happy or sad. Using 'Talking Ted', have a round of:

"I am happy when _____ ."

Closing Phase

End by singing together:

If you're happy and you know it...Clap your hands, Stamp your feet, Shout, "I am."
If you're happy and you know it and you really want to show it
If you're happy and you know it...

Further Activities

Have a special 'happy cloak/hat', that children can wear if they are feeling sad. Everyone must be kind to the wearer to cheer her up.

Make a collage of 'Things that make us happy' to display on the wall.

Golden Rules

Learning Objectives

To maintain attention, concentrate and sit quietly, work as part of a group, understand that there need to be agreed values and codes of behaviour, understand what is right and wrong and why.

Resources

A display poster of the Golden Rules (these are the moral values that you wish to promote and can be pinned up on the wall). The Golden Rules advocated by the Jenny Mosley Quality Circle Time Model are:

Do be gentle, don't hurt anybody

Do be kind and helpful, don't hurt people's feelings

Do be honest, don't cover up the truth

Do work hard, don't waste time

Do look after property, don't waste or damage things

Do listen to people, don't interrupt

(See Resources section for how to obtain posters of the Golden Rules.) If you feel that the wording is too difficult for the children to understand, then just concentrate on the first three, including the others gradually.

Two glove puppets.

Introductory Phase

Introduce the two puppets to the children by name, e.g.
Harry Hedgehog, Rosie Rabbit. Tell the children that Rosie wants to talk to them. Rosie says:

> "Harry Hedgehog is making me feel very sad. He hits me and calls me nasty names. He won't share anything with me and he breaks my toys. I don't think he knows how to be kind."

Middle Phase

Using hands up to answer, ask the children if they think that Harry Hedgehog should be doing these things. Ask the children why. Discuss with the children how Harry Hedgehog should behave. What could they do if Harry Hedgehog didn't know how to be good – perhaps they could tell and show him. Display the poster of the Golden Rules for everyone to see. Go through each one to make sure that the children understand them. Tell the children that if everyone follows the Golden Rules at nursery, it will be a happy place for all of them.

Closing Phase

Ask the children to hold hands around the circle and sing with you (to the tune of 'London Bridge is Falling Down'):

> We will keep our Golden Rules, Golden Rules, Golden Rules.
>
> We will keep our Golden Rules, to make our nursery happy.

Further Activities

Divide the children into small groups and let them role-play situations in which they can practise being kind and helpful, e.g. pretend that you are a child that has been hurt, a child who feels sad, or a child who has no one to play with. Help them with the dialogue they might use.

Photocopy the Golden Rules for each child and ask them to colour in the background using 'happy' colours. They can then take their copies home.

All About Me

Learning Objectives

To have an awareness of their own views and feelings, personal affirmation.

Resources

A box with a mirror placed inside. Talking object.

Introductory Phase

Say to the children that you have a box and when you look inside you can see someone special. Ask if they would like to see the special person. Say to the children that they must keep very quiet as they pass the box round and not say who the special person is until everyone has had a look.

Ask the children who the special person is. When they answer "Me!" tell them that they are right, they are all special.

Middle Phase

Play a game of changing places by category, e.g.:

"Anyone who has a dog, likes ice cream, likes the colour blue" etc.

Closing Phase

Using 'Talking Ted', end with a round of:

"I am good at _____ ."

If a child cannot think of anything, invite the other children to offer a suggestion.

Further Activities

Create a special 'Golden Chair' by painting a chair gold and
placing a cushion on it. Choose a different child each week to sit on the chair.
Keep a good piece of work completed by the child to show to the other children.
The other children can make positive statements about the child in the chair
such as:

> "Sasha is good at running, she has pretty hair, she smiles a lot, she is helpful at
> tidying up."

Photocopy a shield for each child with various headings and help them fill it in.
Display the shields on the wall.

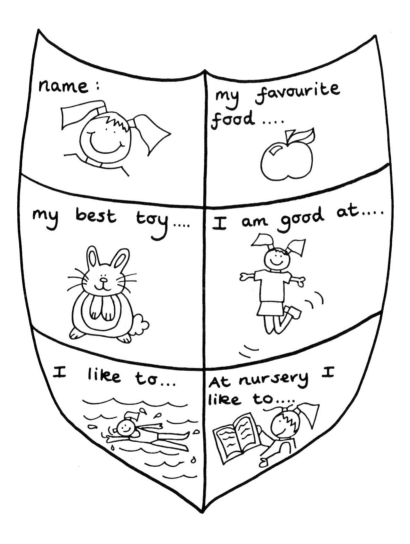

My Friend

Learning Objectives

To have a developing awareness of their own needs, views and feelings and be sensitive to the needs, views and feelings of others. To form good relationships with peers.

Resources

Two photographs of friends of yours. Two soft toys or glove puppets. Talking object.

Introductory Phase

Show the photographs to the children and tell them that they are your friends. Ask the children if they have friends. Ask them what is nice about having friends. Ask the children why it is good to be friendly to others.

Middle Phase

Introduce the puppets or toys to the children:

> "Hello children, I'd like you to meet Harry Hedgehog and Maisie Mouse.
> They are friends.
> What sort of things do you think they might do together?"

E.g. play with toys together, share sweets, go for a walk, give each other a hug. Mime the activities with the toys talking through the actions. The children can also mime the activities with a partner in the centre of the circle.

Closing Phase

Using 'Talking Ted', end with a round of:

> "I like friends because _____ ."

Further Activities

Encourage the children to work with different partners so that they get to know each other. It is also a good idea for them to sit by different children in the circle.

Encourage friendliness by giving stickers or a certificate to a child who has been friendly to another, stating 'You are a kind friend'.

Ask the children to draw a picture of their friends.

Sharing

Learning Objectives

To have a developing awareness of the needs and feelings of others, to respond to significant experiences, showing a range of feelings when appropriate.

Resources

Two glove puppets. A small selection of toys.

Introductory Phase

Introduce the puppets to the children, e.g. Harry Hedgehog and Sita Squirrel.

Sita Squirrel has a pile of toys in front of her. Play out the following dialogue with the puppets:

You	"Harry Hedgehog, why are you looking so sad today?"
Harry	"Sita won't let me share the toys with her. I've got nothing to play with."
You	"Sita, why won't you share the toys with Harry Hedgehog?"
Sita	"Because I had them first."
You	"But Sita, you can't play with all the toys at once and poor Harry Hedgehog has no toys."

Ask the children if they think that Sita is right. What should Sita do? Why should Sita share?

You	"Sita, you have heard what the children have said, now what do you think?"
Sita	"I think they are right. It is kind to share and I want to be kind. I will let Harry Hedgehog have some."

Sita gives some toys to Harry.

Middle Phase

Tell the children that they are going to pretend to do some sharing.
They are to imagine that they have their very favourite sweets in a bag. Think about taking one of these delicious sweets and popping it into their mouth. Imagine the lovely taste. Now they are going to be kind and pretend to offer their sweets to other children. (Each child has a turn to offer to two other children). Remind children to say thank you when they have taken a sweet. They then pretend to eat and enjoy the sweet.

Closing Phase

Pass a hand-shake around the circle.

Further Activities

Make a point of emphasising the idea of sharing and turn-taking when opportunities arise. This also applies to sharing jobs such as tidying up.

Draw round a child's hand and use it to write a commendation on for sharing. This is called a 'Helping Hands' award.

Being Kind

Learning Objectives

To be sensitive to the feelings of others, consider the consequences of their words.

Resources

Two glove puppets or soft toys. A talking object.

Introductory Phase

Introduce the toys, e.g. Daisy Doll and Teddy. Tell the children that Daisy is crying because Teddy has called her a nasty name. Ask the children if they think Teddy was right to do that. Why not? Establish with the children that saying unkind things hurts people's feelings. What should Teddy do now? Say that he is sorry. Act this out with advice from the children as to what Teddy should say.

Middle Phase

Ask the children to tell you actions that are kind e.g. sharing, helping someone when they are hurt, saying nice things to people etc.

Choose two or three of the suggestions and let the children mime the actions in the middle of the circle with a partner.

Closing Phase

Ask the children to think of one kind thing that they could do for someone e.g. helping mummy, letting a brother/sister share toys etc. Using 'Talking Ted' end with a round of:

"I will be kind and _____ ."

Further Activities

Kindness tree: Plant a bare twig into a pot. Make cut-outs of leaves and when a child has done something kind, write the child's name and the deed on a leaf and attach it to the twig.

Make a wallchart with the children under the headings Kind/Unkind. Use gold backing behind the kind words, but a dull background for the unkind words. For example:

KIND	UNKIND
Share	Kick
Take turns	Push
Help	Call names
Friendly	Bossy

Head to Toes

Learning Objectives

Work as part of a group, take turns, learn and practise body parts.

Resources

Prior to Circle Time, make a cassette recording of each child saying a few sentences about something they like doing. A talking object.

Introductory Phase

Using the traditional rhyme

Tommy Thumb, Tommy Thumb, where are you?,

substitute the first two words (repeated) for each child's name. The child replies,

"Here I am, here I am"

to which you respond,

"How do you do!"

Continue around the circle until all the children have had a turn.

Middle Phase

Play the cassette of the children's voices. Ask them to guess who each one is. They must put up their hands to guess, no shouting out.

Closing Phase

Placing both hands on the body parts named, say the following rhyme with the children:

Heads and shoulders, knees and toes, knees and toes,
Heads and shoulders, knees and toes, knees and toes.
Eyes and ears and mouth and nose,
Heads and shoulders, knees and toes.

Using 'Talking Ted', end with a round of:

"I like my _____ (name one body part)."

Further Activities

On a large sheet of paper, draw round the body shape of each child. Let the children draw in hair, face etc.

In pairs, the children study their partner's features and describe them to you e.g. colour of hair, eyes, shape of face, length of hair etc.

Megan has long brown hair and blue eyes. She has......

Body Movements

Learning Objectives

To work as part of a group, learn about body parts.

Resources

None.

Introductory Phase

Read the following extract to the children and act out each body movement:

> Heads nod
>
> Eyes blink
>
> Mouths snap (open and shut)
>
> Necks bend
>
> Shoulders lift
>
> Arms raise
>
> Fingers wiggle
>
> Waists turn
>
> Hips sway
>
> Knees bend
>
> Feet jump

Middle Phase

Ask the children what they use various body parts for. The children respond by saying and miming an appropriate action, e.g.

> "I use my eyes to see with, my feet to walk/run/jump, my hands to play with."

Closing Phase

Read the following extract to the children and act out each body movement ending with the children being still and quiet.

> I wriggle my fingers
> I wriggle my toes
> I wriggle my shoulders
> and I wriggle my nose
> when there are no more
> wriggles left in me
> I am as still as I can be

Further Activities

Have a brainstorming session with the children to see how many activities they can think of which involve using their hands.

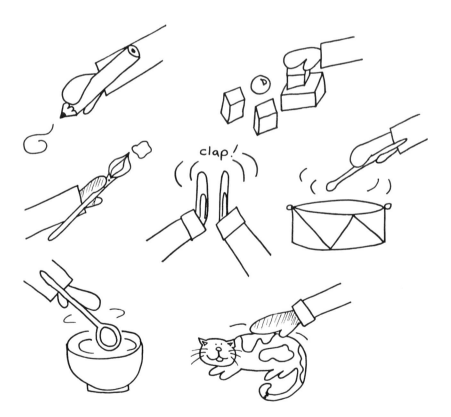

See how many different ways they can think of moving their feet, e.g. walking, running, shuffling, on tip-toe, jumping etc.

This is the Way we Brush our Hair

Learning Objectives

To practise dressing and undressing independently, manage personal hygiene.

Resources

Dressing up clothes – you will need three to four items for each child. Choose these according to age and ability of the children.

Introductory Phase

Tell the children that they are going to mime getting up and getting dressed. Ask them to tell you what they do and in what order, then talk them through the mimes.

Middle Phase

Put the dressing-up clothes into the centre of the circle. Specify to the children what they have to find and put on, e.g. a hat, a jumper, skirt/trousers and a jacket. Tell the children that you want to see how quickly they can find and put on the items.

Closing Phase

Sing with the children and mime the actions to

> Here we go round the mulberry bush on a cold and frosty morning.

Include actions such as:

> This is the way we wash our face
> This is the way we brush our hair
> This is the way we clean our teeth.

When the children are 'ready', they sit down very quietly with arms folded and legs crossed.

Further Activities

Have a selection of fasteners for the children to practise on, e.g. zips, buttons, velcro, laces etc.

Play a game with the children where they take their shoes off and put them in the middle of the circle in a pile. Let each child, in turn, go into the centre and select their shoes from the pile.

Different Faces

Learning Objectives

To understand that there are people with different views and cultures from their own which need to be treated with respect, and to understand that they can expect others to treat their views and cultures with respect.

Resources

Masks of different ethnic groups, e.g. African, Chinese, Eskimo, Asian. Nordic; (you can make these yourself by pasting magazine illustrations onto card). A mirror. A suitable book from the nursery library about the life of a child in another country, e.g. 'One big family' by Ifeoma Onyefulu, publ. Frances Lincoln.

Introductory Phase

Let the children pass the 'faces' around and look at them. If any children want to, they can try on the masks and look at their reflections in the mirror.

Middle Phase

Ask the children what differences there are between the faces, e.g. hair, skin colour, shape of eyes. Tell the children that there are lots of different people living in the world. What else might be different about them – food, language, clothing, houses? Older children may consider religion and culture.

Ask the children what is the same about all people, e.g. they all need food, somewhere to live, friends and family. They all have feelings. Prompt the children to recognise that in some ways all people are the same.

Closing Phase

Read your chosen library book.

Further Activities

Try and arrange for visitors of different races and cultures to come in and talk to the children and bring in items of interest such as different food, costume, religious artefacts.

The Six Areas of Learning

2. Communication, Language and Literacy

'The development and use of communication is at the heart of young children's learning... The ability to communicate gives children the capacity to participate more fully in their society' – QCA Curriculum Guidance

Learning objectives covered in this section are:

♦ Enjoy listening to and using spoken and written language, and readily turn to it in their play and learning

♦ Listen with enjoyment and respond to stories, songs and rhymes

♦ Use language to imagine and recreate roles and experiences

♦ Use talk to organise, sequence and clarify thinking, ideas, feelings and events

♦ Sustain attentive listening, responding to what they have heard by relevant comments, questions or actions

♦ Interact with others, negotiating plans and activities and taking turns in conversation

♦ Extend their vocabulary

♦ Re-tell narratives in the correct sequence

♦ Speak clearly and audibly with confidence and control and show awareness of the listener

♦ Hear and say initial sounds in words

♦ Link sounds to letters, naming and sounding the letters in the alphabet

♦ Read a range of familiar and common words

♦ Attempt writing for various purposes

♦ Write their own names and other things such as captions

♦ Use their phonic knowledge to write simple words

Toy Tales

Learning Objectives

To use language to imagine roles, respond to stories, speak clearly and audibly and listen attentively.

Resources

A selection of story books about toys, e.g. Noddy, Paddington Bear, Sooty, Winnie the Pooh, enough to share one between two children.

Introductory Phase

Arrange the children in pairs. Share the books out. Let each pair look at their book together and tell each other if they know anything about the character. You can demonstrate how to do this with your partner (a helper).

Middle Phase

Tell the children that you are a magician and you are going to turn them into various toys. They can mime the actions of each toy in the centre of the circle. Tell them that when you clap twice they must stop and stand still until you turn them into a different toy, e.g. train, toy dog, robot, ball, puppet, toy mouse.

Closing Phase

Using 'Talking Ted' end with a round of:

"If I were a toy I would be _____ because _____ ."

Further Activities

This circle session can be repeated using animal stories instead.

Create a toy shop in the class room. The children can take turns at being a customer or a sales assistant.

Using available costumes, make up a play in which the children pretend to be toys in a playroom. They come alive at night and go back to sleep at daylight. The children could perform their play to other classes or their parents.

The Letter 'D'

Learning Objectives

To hear and say initial sounds in words, link sounds to letters, naming and sounding the letter of the alphabet.

Resources

A selection of objects or illustrations beginning with the letter D, e.g. dog, doll, drum, dish, duck, dinosaur, donkey, deer, doughnut. A large piece of card showing the letters Dd.

Introductory Phase

Show the visual aids to the children. Ask them to name each item. Ask them if anyone can say the beginning sound of each word – repeat the name several times if necessary emphasising the beginning letter sound.

Middle Phase

Ask if any child knows the name of the letter that makes this sound. Show the letter card. Ask the children if they can think of any other words beginning with the letter D. Lay out the cards in the middle of the circle. Invite each child to go into the circle, choose a card and say:

"I like the d _____ because _____ ."

Closing Phase

Tell the children you are all going to say some words beginning with the letter D, e.g. Daisy Doll dances, Daffy Duck likes doughnuts. The children repeat after you. Say together the nursery rhyme:

> Diddle diddle dumpling my son John
> Went to bed with his trousers on
> One sock off and one sock on
> Diddle diddle dumpling my son John

Further Activities

Think of as many ways as possible for the children to 'write' the letter D or d, e.g. by joining dots, with blocks on the floor, using large brushes and paint, chalk large letters on the floor or use large cut-outs for the children to walk round, in the sand tray.

Make a display table of objects beginning with the letter D. The children can bring in items from home as well. Repeat with other letters.

Interesting Objects

Learning Objectives

To speak clearly and audibly, organise ideas, extend descriptive vocabulary and listen attentively.

Resources

Enough interesting objects for one per child and one for your self. Choose items for their colour, texture and shape, e.g. a shell, a pine cone, tree bark, brightly coloured beads, some moss. Put all the objects into a box.

Introductory Phase

Ask each child in turn to come and take an object from the box and take one yourself.

Middle Phase

Explain to the children that you want them to think of words which tell you about their object. Describe yours first as an example. You can prompt the children with appropriate questions so that you get responses like

"hard, soft, shiny, fluffy, bright, prickly, long, thin."

Encourage each child to think of two words to describe their object then ask the other children if they know any more. You can then introduce some new descriptive vocabulary.

Closing Phase

Depending on the objects that you have chosen, select a few categories that some, but not all of the objects will fit into, e.g. anything that is soft, hard, round, brown. Call out a category. If their object fits into that category the children can stand up and hold them out for all to see. They then sit down again and a different category is called.

Further Activities

Make a display table of contrasting objects e.g. soft/hard, dull/shiny.

Go out on a walk and collect interesting natural objects to talk about. Place several items on a plain coloured tray and show them to the children. Ask the children to close their eyes then remove one item and ask the children to guess what is missing.

Nutty Nursery Rhymes

Learning Objectives

To encourage the children to listen attentively, respond with spoken language and retell narratives in the correct sequence.

Resources

A book of nursery rhymes, e.g. the 'Puffin Book of Rhymes' or 'Ladybird Book of Rhymes'.

Introductory Phase

Tell the children that you are going to read some favourite nursery rhymes, but you sometimes get them wrong and you need their help. Choose two or three familiar rhymes and say them a line at a time inserting incorrect words. Allow the children to correct your mistakes for you. Then say the rhyme correctly together with the children. For example:

> Humpty Bumpty sat on a chair
>
> Jack and Jill went up a mountain

Middle Phase

Ask if any of the children would like to stand up and say a nursery rhyme to the others. Allow the children to prompt if anyone needs help.

Closing Phase

Read two or three more familiar rhymes.
Leave words out for the children to supply, then say them together with the children, e.g.:

> Baa baa _____ sheep have you any _____ .

Further Activities

Divide the children into small groups of four or five with an adult supervisor to

each group. Allow the children to choose a nursery rhyme and mime actions to it while a child or practitioner says the rhyme. They can discuss the appropriate actions between themselves. Each group can perform their rhyme to the other children.

Work with rhyming words, e.g. matching words on cards which rhyme, thinking of words which rhyme with a given word.

Show and Tell

Learning objectives

To use talk to organise, sequence and clarify ideas, sustain attentive listening and take turns in speaking. To speak clearly and audibly.

Resources

Ask each child to bring in a favourite object. This can be a toy, video, game, etc. Inform the parents also of this request to avoid children being left out because they have forgotten or could not find anything suitable. It might also be a good idea to ask parents to talk about the object with the child prior to the Circle Time. Ask the practitioners to bring in a favourite object too. It may be a good idea, especially for younger children, to divide the class into smaller groups so that the activities do not take too long and become boring.

Introductory Phase

Ask each child in turn to show their object and say why they like it. It might be a good idea if an adult has the first turn to demonstrate what to do. Two or three sentences will suffice. After each child has spoken, make a positive comment such as:

> "That looks great fun."

> "That looks very interesting."

> "What a lovely colour!"

Say to the children:

> "Now we would all like to say thank you _____ ." (insert child's name)

Middle Phase

You now show your favourite object and ask the children to try and guess why you like it, using hands up to answer. You can add any further reasons.

Closing Phase

Ask the children one at a time to put their objects in the centre of the circle. Join hands around the circle and walk around the objects as you say in a slow, measured rhythm:

> "We've brought in / all our favourite things / to share with everyone . / Thank you everybody / for making it / good fun."

The children can then say the rhyme with you.

Further Activities

Make up a display table of everyone's favourite things with their names alongside. Invite parents, other classes and supervisors to come and look at it. Make models, collages or drawings of other favourite things.

My Favourite Book

Learning Objectives

To discuss stories, respond with relevant comments and listen attentively.

Resources

Ask the children (with prior prompts to parents) to bring in a favourite book from home. If a child fails to do this, ensure that an adult who is familiar with the child helps the child to choose a book s/he has enjoyed from the nursery library. Also bring in a suitable favourite book to read to the children. It may be a good idea, especially with younger children, to divide the class into smaller groups for the introductory phase.

Introductory Phase

Ask each child in turn to show the book s/he has brought in. Ask the child why he likes the book. Ask if any of the other children have read the book and what comments they have. Try to make a positive comment about each book such as:

> "That book was very exciting/funny."

> "The pictures in that book are very good."

> "I liked the bit where _____ ."

Middle Phase

Show the children your favourite book and then read it to them.

Closing Phase

Ask the children to put up their hands and say why they thought you really liked that book. You can add further reasons to the ones they suggest.

Further Activities

The children can paint/draw a picture from their chosen books.

They could have a dressing-up day and come to nursery in the costume of a book character. The other children could try to guess who they were. Get in touch with your local library to arrange a visit with your class. Alternatively, some libraries have a scheme where the librarian will visit your premises to talk to the children.

We're the same

Learning Objectives

Link sounds to letters, read a range of familiar and common words. Writing practice.

Resources

A selection of simple common nouns with corresponding illustrations, e.g. cat, dog, ball, cup, car, bag.

Slips of card to cover the name. These can be fixed with sticky tack.

Two sets of cards with a noun printed on each card to match the illustrations. A bag or covered box.

Introductory Phase

Put the two sets of cards into the bag/box and give them a shake. Display the visual aids, using three to six depending on the age of the children, for all the children to see. Invite each child in turn to select a card from the bag. The child shows the card to the other children and, if able, says the word. If not, the other children are invited to try. Then read the word to the children and ask them to repeat it. The child then places the card next to the correct visual aid.

Middle Phase

Return the cards to the bag. Cover up the noun on the illustrations with your card slips. Invite the children to repeat the previous activity and see if they can place their cards by the correct illustration. The other children can offer help where necessary.

Closing Phase

Collect in the cards again and select enough pairs to go around the circle, i.e. six children, three pairs of cards. If there is an odd number of children, retain one card for yourself. Distribute the cards face down to the children ensuring that pairs are not with consecutive children. Ask the children to look at their cards and find their partners with matching cards. When they have found their partners, they can show and say their words together to the rest of the circle.

Further Activities

Older children can copy some of the words.

Build up the words together from the individual letters. Older children can try independently.

Magic Moments

Learning Objectives

To use language to imagine roles, use talk to sequence ideas, sustain attentive listening, interact with others, speak clearly and audibly and show awareness of the listener.

Resources

A wizard's pointed hat, a wand.

Introductory Phase

Tell the children that today they are going to think about magic and wishes. Begin with a game of Winnie Witch Says (played as Simon Says) during which you wear the wizard's hat and hold the wand.

Middle Phase

Discuss with the children how wonderful it would be if they could wish for nice things for everyone, e.g.:

> "I wish it was always warm and sunny at the weekend."

> "I wish everyone had a sweet tree in their garden."

> "I wish no one was ever ill."

Ask the children if any of them would like to wear the wizard's hat and hold the wand and make a nice wish for everyone; (they can only make one wish at a time). After each wish say with all the children:

> "Thank you _____ for your kind wish."

Closing Phase

Select a suitable book from your library with a magical theme to read to the children, e.g. one of the Mog books by Helen Nicoll and Jan Pienkowski published by Picture Puffin.

Further Activities

The children can make and decorate wizards' hats to take home.

See if you can organise a magician to come in and do a show for the children.

Shopping Day

Learning Objectives

Use language to imagine roles, use talk to sequence ideas, respond to what they have heard by relevant comments, interact with others, take turns in conversation, speak clearly and audibly.

Resources

A small coffee table for the centre of the circle. Twenty grocery items, e.g. vegetables, fruit, cereals, toiletries. These can be real, from the nursery playhouse resources or cut-out adverts pasted onto card. A shallow cardboard box. You may wish to split the class into groups of four to six for the first two phases. If you feel that these activities would be too difficult for your group, you can just ask the children to name items with you and then say what they would like to buy if they went shopping.

Introductory Phase

Place the grocery items in the centre of the circle, along with the box. Child One goes to the centre, selects an item, places it in the box, returns to her seat and says:

"I went shopping and bought a _____ ."

Child Two repeats this action and names her item plus the one already in the box. Child Three repeats the action and names her item plus the two already in the box, and so on. Any child who cannot remember all the items can look in the box. At the end say with all the children:

"We went shopping and bought _____ "

naming all the items. This game can be played several times, beginning each game with a different child and new items.

Middle Phase

Place the table in the centre of the circle. Tell the children they are going to pretend to go shopping. Decide with the children what the shop will be, e.g. a bakery. Discuss what items would be in a bakery: loaves, rolls, cakes, pies. One child will be the shopkeeper, e.g. Mr/Mrs Bun the Baker, the others will be customers. The baker stands on one side of the table and each child in turn goes to the baker's to buy one to three items depending on age. The customer says:

"Please Mr Bun may I have _____ ."

Mr Bun mimes getting the items and putting them in bags saying each item as he hands it to the customer. The customer mimes paying the money and says:

"Thank you Mr Bun. Goodbye."

The customer returns to his seat and the next child goes shopping. It may be a good idea to demonstrate the procedure to the children with a helper. You can change the shopkeeper or type of shop as you wish.

Closing Phase

The following story has four cue words repeated in the text. Each time a cue word is read the children have to respond with a particular action:

Bun   – put hands on head.

Loaf   – tap knees twice.

Cake   – stand up, turn round, sit down.

Pie   – all move one seat to the right.

Choose two to four cues depending on age. Use helpers to prompt the children with the correct actions. Rehearse the words and actions a few times. Pause briefly after each cue word.

"Hello Mr. Bun ... I have a very long shopping list today.
I'd like a brown loaf ... and a white loaf ...
and six currant buns ... a nice big vegetable pie ...
and a small cottage loaf ...
Now let me see. What else do I need? Oh yes,
four plain buns ... a large cream cake ...
a crusty loaf ... and one of your delicious apple pies ...
Please can you make me a birthday cake ... for Danny next Tuesday and save me a
sliced loaf ... and a savoury mince pie ...
That's all. Thank you Mr. Bun ... Goodbye."

Further Activities

Arrange a visit to several different types of shop with small groups of children
e.g. a butcher's, a newsagent's, a greengrocer's.

Try and arrange to take the children to a bakery to see how bread, cakes etc
are made.

Set up a type of shop in the play area using nursery materials and items brought
in from home.

Fantasy Journey

Learning Objectives

To imagine and create role play, sustain attentive listening, responding with relevant actions.

Resources

None, but part of this session will take place outside the circle.

Introductory Phase

Tell the children that they are going to play a game. Each child in turn says:

> "Car", "bus" or "lorry"

in that sequence around the circle. The children stand up to play the game. If any child gets the sequence wrong, she is out and must sit down. Practise saying the words in the correct sequence a few times with the children. See how fast the children can say the words.

Ask the children if they enjoy going on journeys. Ask them where they have been and how they have travelled.

Tell the children that today they are going on a pretend journey. You will tell them all about the journey as they go along and they must mime the appropriate actions.

Middle Phase

Read the following extract. Use adult helpers to lead the children and demonstrate the mimes outside the circle.

> Before we go on our journey we must make sure that we have everything that we will need. We will start by packing our backpacks. Put your backpack on the floor and open it up. Now we will put in some food and drink, a torch, our sleeping bags and a thick jumper in case it gets cold. Pick up your backpacks and put them on your backs.

Right, off we go. We are going to walk across a field, but first we have to climb over a stile. Be careful where you tread in the field - there are stinging nettles and you don't want to get stung. It's starting to get very hot and the heat is making you feel tired and thirsty. You begin to walk slower and slower, slower and slower.

Suddenly you see a stream. You take off your backpacks, sit down by the stream, take off your shoes and socks and dip your feet into the cool water, then you take your food and drink out of your backpack and have a picnic.

Time to carry on. Put on your socks and shoes, pick up your backpack and off we go again. We're walking through a wood now. There are fallen trees to climb over and sometimes the branches are low and you have to duck down to go under them. Carefully move the prickly brambles out of your way. The bushes are so thick now that you will have to get down on your hands and knees to crawl through them.

At last you are out of the wood. It's getting dark and cold. You will have to get your jumpers out of your backpacks and your torches. Shine your torches in front of you so that you can see where you are going. There is a big hill to climb. It's so steep you are puffing and panting. You climb higher and higher. Your legs are very tired. You are at the top of the hill and here is your camp site. You take your sleeping bags out of your backpacks and lay them on the ground. Then you climb in, close your eyes and go to sleep.

Closing Phase

Ask the children to return to the circle. Using 'Talking Ted', end with a round of:

"The part I liked best was _____ ."

Further Activities

Use chairs to make a bus. All sit on the bus and sing the song 'The wheels on the bus go round and round'.

Make a wall display of all the different modes of transport, e.g. car, bus, lorry, train, plane, boat.

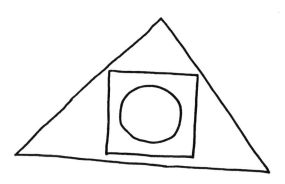

The Six Areas of Learning

3. Mathematical Development

'Children's mathematical development arises out of daily experiences in a rich and interesting environment' – QCA Curriculum Guidance

Learning objectives covered in this section are:

♦ Say and use number names in order in familiar contexts

♦ Count reliably up to ten everyday objects

♦ Recognise numerals 1 to 9

♦ Use language such as 'more' or 'less', 'greater' or 'smaller', 'heavier' or 'lighter', to compare two numbers or quantities

♦ In practical activities and discussion begin to use the vocabulary involved in adding and subtracting

♦ Find one more or one less than a number from 1 to 10

♦ Talk about, recognise and recreate simple patterns

♦ Use language such as 'circle' or 'bigger' to describe the shape and size of solids and flat shapes

♦ Use everyday words to describe position

♦ Use developing mathematical ideas and methods to solve practical problems

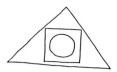

Let's Count Together

Learning Objectives

To practise counting, use vocabulary involved in subtraction, practise naming colours.

Resources

Make some play-dough or card currant buns. The number of buns you require will depend on the age of the children and how far you can expect them to count, between three and ten. The same number each of red, yellow and blue bricks in a bag.

Introductory Phase

Lay out the currant buns in the centre of the circle. Count with the children how many there are. All say the traditional rhyme,

> (Five) currant buns in the baker's shop
> Big and round with a cherry on the top
> Along came (Joe) with a penny one day
> Bought a currant bun and took it away.

Choose a child to remove one bun, then count together how many are left. Repeat with different children until there are no buns left in the centre.

Middle Phase

Pass round the bag and let each child take out one brick. Put the bricks, one at a time, in colour sets in the centre of the circle, naming the colour each time. Count how many bricks are in each set.

Closing Phase

Say the traditional counting rhyme:

> One, two, buckle my shoe etc.

Mime the actions and encourage the children to say the numbers with you if they are able.

Further Activities

Teach the children other traditional counting rhymes such as:

Ten fat sausages sizzling in a pan.

Five little ducks went swimming one day.

One, two, three, four, five, once I caught a fish alive.

Five little speckled frogs.

A useful resource is 'Fun Counting Songs', a cassette produced by Fast Forward Music Promotions Limited.

Use counting in practical or play situations, e.g. laying out plates and cups, counting a given number of jumps, taking a given number of steps.

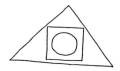

Helping Sita

Learning Objectives

To recognise numerals.

Resources

A glove puppet.

A large number line, say three to nine depending on the age of the children.

Numerals on cards which correspond to the number line.

Introductory Phase

Introduce a puppet such as Sita Squrrel to the children. Sita shows the number line to the children. She asks them what it is and what is written on it. Sita says she would like to learn the numbers and asks the children if they would help her.

Read the numerals on the number line twice with the children. Sita would like a go. She makes some mistakes and forgets some numbers, allowing the children to prompt with the correct answer. Sita asks the children to read the number line with her once more.

Middle Phase

Put the number line in the centre of the circle. Give each child a number card. The children take turns to look at their number, say it aloud then place it on the number line. Sita has a turn and asks the children to help her.

Closing Phase

Play a game as you put the cards away. Choose a child and clap a number such as three. The child must pick up a card with the numeral 3 on and put it away. Continue like this until every child has had a turn and all the cards have gone.

Further Activities

Create opportunities to recognise and practise numerals. Walk round large numerals on the floor, paint inside the outlines of numerals, show a different numeral each day at the beginning and end of the day.

Put numerals in random sequence. Ask the children to put them in the correct sequence first using a number line, then without.

Make and eat gingerbread numerals.

Circles, Squares and Triangles

Learning Objectives

Use language to describe shapes, practise names of colours.

Resources

Circles, squares and triangles in sets of different colours printed onto cards.

One large card with the three shapes.

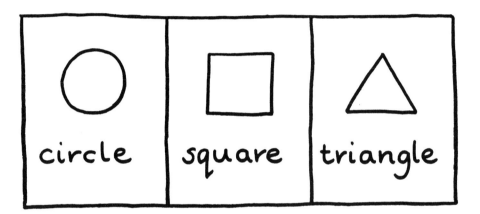

Introductory Phase

Place the card with the three shapes in the circle for all the children to see. Ask the children if they know what each shape is called. Practise saying the names together. Call out different shapes at random. The children can volunteer to point to the correct shape on the card. Do this two or three times for each shape.

Middle Phase

Give each child a shape card. The children take turns to show their card, name the shape and place it on the corresponding shape on the large shape card in the circle.

Closing Phase

Put away the shapes by calling out the colour and name, e.g. blue square, red circle.

Further Activities

Make up a wall or table display of these shapes in the environment:

Circle   –   sun, plate, ball, watch face.

Square   –   book, paper, t.v. screen.

Triangle –   roof, Toblerone chocolate, half a slice of toast.

Play snap with the shape cards. Construct things with small building bricks in the shapes of triangles, squares and circles.

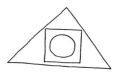

Shapes and Patterns

Learning Objectives

Use language to describe shapes, create sets, create simple patterns.

Resources

At least five different coloured sets of circle, square and triangle cards; (three different colours will be enough for younger children).

A cassette player and tape of music.

Introductory Phase

Shuffle the cards and give them out, one to each child. Ask the children to hold up their cards if they have a circle, then square, then triangle. Create different sets in the centre of the circle by either shape or colour categories, e.g. 'any blue shape', 'any coloured square'. The older children can decide on the different sets themselves.

Middle Phase

Let the children make simple repeating patterns with their shapes. They could begin with all circles then perhaps circle, square, circle, square, then two of one shape and one of another. See how inventive they can be.

Closing Phase

Play musical shapes on the same principle as musical statues. When the music stops, whoever moves is out. Instead of calling the child's name call the shape that they are holding, e.g. blue square, red triangle.

Further Activities

Let the children make up their own patterns using potato prints of the three shapes.

Begin some simple sequences on paper for them to continue.

Put coloured bricks or beads in a given sequence.

Bigger and Smaller

Learning Objectives

To use language to compare size.

Resources

Six objects of varying sizes.

Introductory Phase

Ask the children to crouch down on the floor, tuck their heads in and make themselves very small. Tell them that they are gradually going to grow bigger – uncurl, stand up and then stretch up their arms above their heads and grow bigger and bigger. Then they are going to get smaller and smaller and smaller again until they are very small.

Middle Phase

Place the objects in the circle. Pick up two and ask the children which one is bigger. Repeat with two more and ask which object is smaller. Ask the children to help you put the objects in order of size. Say as you do this, "small, bigger, bigger, bigger" etc. Then looking at the objects from the largest say, "big, smaller, smaller, smaller" etc. If the children are able, also use biggest and smallest.

Closing Phase

Choose two children. Ask "Who is bigger?" Say "Tom is bigger". Repeat with "Who is smaller?" Do this a few times. Put the children in order of height. Older children can say:

"I am bigger than _____ and smaller than _____ ."

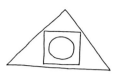

Further Activities

Make up two headings of bigger and smaller. Give the children sets of illustrations to place under the correct headings, such as:

mouse, elephant

shed, house

fruit, tree

Ask the children to draw bigger and smaller, e.g. a big balloon, a smaller balloon, a small person, a bigger person.

Make a wall chart plotting the heights of the children at various times during the year.

Ask the children to make bigger and smaller shapes with play-dough.

More or Less

Learning Objectives

To use language to compare two numbers or quantities, practise counting.

Resources

Choose some items that the children are interested in, e.g. wrapped sweets.

Two soft toys, e.g. a doll and a teddy.

Items suitable for the closing phase activities. Building bricks.

Introductory Phase

Say to the children that you are going to give the teddy and doll some sweets. Make two piles of sweets in front of the toys giving the teddy three sweets and the doll five. Say to the children:

> "Let's count the sweets."

Ask the children who has more sweets. Say together:

> "The doll has more sweets."

Then ask the children who has fewer sweets and say together:

> "Teddy has fewer sweets."

For younger children, just use "more".

Middle Phase

Give two children a different number of bricks to build a tower. Count the bricks in each tower and ask the children whose tower has more bricks. Ask them to say with you:

> "_____'s tower has more bricks and _____'s tower has fewer bricks."

Repeat this with different children and a different number of bricks.

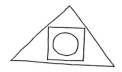

Closing Phase

Think of ways of getting the children to respond with the words more or fewer/less, e.g. share a drink between teddy and the doll giving one only a very small amount and ask the children if that is fair.

Prepare a packed lunch for either toy giving one much more etc.

Further Activities

Ask the children to divide objects into groups of more and fewer.

Use addition and subtraction language with older children, e.g. begin with two groups of equal amounts and say:

"If I take two away / add two, which group has more / fewer?"

Heavier and Lighter

Learning Objectives

To use language to compare objects.

Resources

A selection of small objects of different weights.

A set of balancing scales.

Two bags of lentils of equal weight.

Additional lentils.

A glove puppet.

Introductory Phase

Place the scales and objects in the circle (on a low table if you prefer). Introduce the puppet, e.g. Harry Hedgehog. Harry looks at the scales, he asks the children if anyone knows what they are for. Harry talks to the children as he places different objects on the scales and watches them go up and down. He asks the children if they can think of the reason why this happens. The side that goes down is heavier. The other side lighter.

Middle Phase

Ask a child to choose two of the objects and place them on the scales. Which object is heavier and which is lighter? Say this with the children. Repeat several times with different children. Put the two equal weights of lentils on the scales. Tell the children that they are the same. Add some lentils to one bag and ask the children why the scales have gone down. Then ask the children how you could make the other side heavier.

Closing Phase

Let the children put the objects away by choosing two to weigh and discarding the lighter object each time.

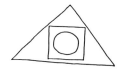

Further Activities

Let the children work in pairs with objects to weigh on the scales. Ask them to guess first which is heavier/lighter and then use the scales.

Use containers with sand on the balancing scales. Ask the children to see if they can make them balance. While they are working use language of heavier/lighter.

Play a game filling a bag with items and see which child can lift the heaviest weight.

Under and Over

Learning Objectives

Use everyday words to describe position.

Resources

Box, cup, bag, chair, teddy, sweet.

Introductory Phase

Play Simon Says with the children using positional words – in, on, under, behind, in front of, up, down, above, e.g.

> Simon says put your hands behind your head.
> Simon says put your hands under your knees.
> Simon says stretch your arms up above your head.
> Simon says kneel down.

Middle Phase

Using the objects place them in different positions and ask the children to tell you where you have put them, e.g. put the sweet under the cup, put the teddy inside the box. Ask the children to place the objects where you tell them, e.g. put the teddy on the chair, put the cup beside the box.

Closing Phase

Say with the children the following rhyme:

> Teddy bear teddy bear turn around,
> Teddy bear teddy bear touch the ground,
> Teddy bear teddy bear reach up high,
> Teddy bear teddy bear touch the sky.

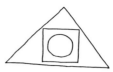

Further Activities

Use apparatus such as chairs, benches, tables, large boxes, tunnels. Tell the children to take up positions inside, under, behind, in front of, etc.

Use positional words to tell the children where to put things when they tidy up.

Let the children use positional words to tell you where to put things.

Money Matters

Learning Objectives

To recognise 1p, 2p and 5p coins. For very young children just use 1p coins and base the activities on what they can manage.

Resources

Use a number of 1p coins corresponding to the children's counting abilities, and some 2p and 5p coins. A selection of objects to buy, e.g. food from the playhouse, books, pencils etc, with prices up to 5p.

Introductory Phase

Look at the coins together. Ask the children if they know what they are – money. Ask the children if they know what their Mummy uses money for.

Talk about the size, colour, shape of the coins and look at the heads and tails pictures and the number depicting the value.

Middle Phase

Tell the children that the coins are called pennies. This is shortened to p when written. Ask the children if they can think why this is. Put down two pennies and count them with the children then show them that the 2p coin has the same value. With older children, repeat this for the 5p. Using the priced objects ask a child to choose something to buy. If, for example, the object costs 3p ask the children to tell you what coins you will need. Older children can suggest different combinations of coins for the same value.

Closing phase

Play a game of 'heads and tails' with the children, asking them to guess which side the coin will land before you flip it. You could count how many times the coin lands on either side, by asking a child to stand on your right if it lands on heads or on your left if it lands on tails.

Further Activities

Do some simple adding or subtracting of 1p from given amounts.

In small groups with an adult helper for each group, let the children suggest some prices for items and then work out the correct coins needed to buy them.

With the parents' consent, organise a sweet shop with sweets priced from 1p to 3p. Let each child have five pennies and buy from the sweet shop. Make rubbings of the coins using paper and wax crayons.

Let's work it out

Learning Objectives

To use developing ideas and methods to solve practical problems.

Resources

A doll. A teddy. Two carrier bags and items to put into the bags. Eight pretend cakes or similar treats. Two balls.

Introductory Phase

Tell the children that you have a special treat for the doll and teddy. In front of the doll place five cakes and in front of teddy place three. Pretend that teddy is talking to you, then tell the children that teddy says it is not fair because the doll has more cakes than he has. Ask the children to count the cakes and then ask them what you could do to make it fair.

Middle Phase

Put all the items into the centre of the circle and tell the children that you are going to put them into the two bags for teddy and the doll to carry. Make one bag much heavier and give this one to the doll. Pretend to listen to the doll then tell the children that the doll has said it isn't fair. Ask the children if they know what the doll means by this and how to make it fair. Let the children sort out the items into the bags making them more equal weights.

Closing Phase

Let the children sort themselves into two teams of equal number. Each team forms a circle and on the command 'go' the children pass a ball round the circle. First team to finish wins. If the circles are too small, use helpers.

Further Activities

Present the children with practical problems they can work on in pairs: dividing items into equal sets, choosing categories to place items in, problems using positional language such as how to reach a high object or move a heavy one.

Set up an obstacle course with the children. Let them go from A to B (this could be where the treasure is hidden) and then describe how they got there.

The Six Areas of Learning

4. Knowledge and Understanding of the World

'Children are developing the crucial knowledge, skills and understanding that help them make sense of the world' – QCA Curriculum Guidance

Learning objectives covered in this section are:

◆ Investigate objects and materials by using all their senses as appropriate

◆ Find out about and identify some features of living things, objects and events they observe

◆ Look closely at similarities, differences, patterns and change

◆ Ask questions about why things happen

◆ Find out about and identify the uses of everyday technology

◆ Find out about past and present events in their own lives

◆ Observe, find out about, and identify features in the place they live and the natural world

◆ Find out about their environment, and talk about those features they like and dislike

Baby Faces

Learning Objectives

To look at and think about age-related changes.

Resources

Ask the parents to provide a photograph of each child as a baby in an envelope with the child's name on.

Introductory Phase

Show the children each photograph in turn. Tell them that if it is their photograph they must not say. Ask the children to guess who each baby is.

Middle Phase

Ask the children how they have changed since they were babies - they have grown, have hair, have teeth, can walk, feed and dress themselves etc.

Closing Phase

Children sing 'Rock-a-bye baby, on the tree top' with miming actions.

Further Activities

Make a table display of baby items, e.g. bottle, bib, rattle, teething ring.

Make a wall display of the baby photos. The children's names can be written under a flap so that people can guess the identities before looking at the names.

Discuss with the children some of the simple age-related changes of adulthood and old age.

Everything Grows

Learning Objectives

To introduce the idea that living things need their own 'food' to grow.

Resources

A pot plant.

Introductory Phase

Let the children look at the plant. Ask them if they know what plants need to help them grow. Tell the children that the plant needs three things:

- ♦ Sunshine

- ♦ Rain

- ♦ Something special in the air that they can't see (called carbon dioxide) – let the children breathe the air in and out.

Choose four children to be 'plants'. They will crouch down in the centre of the circle and be small plants. Tell the other children that they will help the small plants grow into big, strong plants. First they will be the sunshine. Mime a large circular movement with both arms to represent the sun coming out. The children copy this movement as you say;

> Our little plants are in the ground
> Out comes the sun so warm and round.
> It shines on the green leaves all day long,
> And helps our plants grow big and strong.

Tell the small plants that they can grow just a little. Now the children mime the rain falling by moving their arms up and down in front of them and wiggling their fingers while you say:

> Our plants in the ground are thirsty I think
> Down comes the rain and they can drink.

The little plants can grow a bit more, until the children are now standing upright. The other children blow gently to mime the air while you say:

> There's something special in the air
> You can't touch it or see it you know,
> But our plants can't live if it is not there
> Because all of them need it to grow.

The plants now stand up tall and stretch their arms and fingers above their head. Thank the children for helping the little plants to grow big and strong.

Middle Phase

Ask the children if you planted them in the ground would they grow big and strong. Ask them what they need to grow.

Closing Phase

Using 'Talking Ted', end with a round of,

> "My favourite food is _____ ." (no sweets)

Further Activities

The children collect differently shaped leaves and make pictures or do leaf prints.

You could look at a plant more closely with the children in small groups. Talk about the stem and what colour the leaves are and how a plant drinks through its roots. Take a plant out of its pot and show the children the root system. Older children could be introduced to the idea of plants producing fruit to reproduce.

Fruit Basket

Learning Objectives

To investigate objects using their senses, find out about some features of living things.

Resources

A selection of different fruit – including some unusual types – e.g. apples, oranges, bananas, kiwi fruit, star fruit, pomegranate. Some illustrations of the shrubs/trees where the fruits grow.

Introductory Phase

Allow the children to feel, look at and handle their own piece of fruit.

Put the fruit into the middle of the circle and see if the children can find their piece of fruit again.

Middle Phase

Ask the children if they know the names of the fruit. Ask them if they know where fruit comes from. You can show the children the visual aids and tell them that some fruit comes from other countries in ships. Discuss with the children the origin of the fruit from trees and shrubs. With older children, you might like to introduce the idea of the purpose of fruit to the tree.

Closing Phase

Give each child the name apple, orange or plum around the circle. Tell the children that you will call a fruit and the children with that name must stand up and change places. Ensure that the children do know which fruit they are. If you call 'fruit basket' all the children stand and change seats. Warn the children that they must not bump into each other. Use adult helpers where you think prompts might be needed or to ensure sensible behaviour.

Further Activities

Cut up the fruit that you have brought in and let the children
look at and discuss the insides then taste the fruit. They could make a chart to
see which was the most/least popular.

Make a wall display of 'Our fruit basket' with a large card basket filled with
fruit the children have painted.

Wild Animals

Learning Objectives

To find out about and identify some features of common wild animals in Britain.

Resources

Illustrations of wild animals, e.g. mouse, rat, fox, badger, squirrel, rabbit, snake, hedgehog, frog.

Introductory Phase

Ask the children if they have pets at home and what they are. Discuss with the children that some animals aren't kept as pets, but live on their own. Ask the children if they know of any animals that live in the countryside.

Middle Phase

Show the children the visual aids. Ask if they can name the animals. Discuss with the children where the animals might live, e.g. underground burrows, hollow tree trunks, disused buildings, holes in banks, trees. What sorts of thing might these animals eat? Have any children seen any of these animals? Let the children pretend to be some of the animals and mime their actions.

Closing Phase

Choose an animal story from your library to read to the children, e.g. 'Little Tang' by Sally Grindley and John Butler published by Orchard Books.

Further Activities

Using cut-out illustrations and art materials, make a collage of wild animals. Make hedgehogs from clay, with twigs or brown craft matchsticks as bristles. Display the hedgehogs on a table of dried leaves.

Make 'hedgehog' cakes using chocolate sponge mix and chocolate Matchmakers for the spines.

In small groups let the children choose a different animal to do a project on.

This and That

Learning Objectives

To look at objects and identify if they are natural or man-made materials.

Resources

A selection of different objects, e.g. an item made of wood, an item made of stone, a metal object, a plastic beaker, a china cup.

Introductory Phase

Let the children look at and handle the objects, taking care with anything breakable. Discuss with the children the idea that some materials are naturally found in the world around us and some are made by people. Ask them to guess which are made from natural and which from man-made materials (this may be too difficult for younger children). Make two piles in the centre of the circle for the two different categories.

Middle Phase

Discuss with the children where some of the natural materials come from, such as wood from trees, metal from under the ground. With older children you may like to go into further detail of how trees are cut down and sawn into planks or how metal is mined from the ground and has to be smelted before it can be made into goods. You can act out with the children the story of a tree - planting a tree, the tree growing, cutting it down, sawing it into planks etc.

Closing Phase

Using 'Talking Ted', end with a round of:

"My favourite thing was _____ because _____ ."

Further Activities

Try and a visit a timber yard or anywhere local for children to see natural resources being turned into consumables.

Make a project with the children of how a tree is turned into a table.

My Family

Learning Objectives

To think about and discuss 'family' units, but be aware that this may be a sensitive issue for some children such as those with divorced parents.

Resources

Ask the children (with prompts to the parents) to bring in photographs of those they live with, including pets.

Introductory Phase

Split the class into small groups of four or five with an adult to supervise each group. Under the direction of the adult, each child shows their photographs and tells who the 'family' members are. Allow a set time of up to ten minutes for this phase.

Middle Phase

Re-form the class into its usual Circle Time group. Explain to the children that they are going to play a game of changing seats when you call out certain categories such as:

> Anyone with a younger brother/sister
> Anyone with an older brother/sister
> Anyone with a cat/dog/rabbit
> Anyone whose Mummy has black hair
> Anyone whose Daddy wears glasses / has a beard etc
> Anyone who has a 'nan'

When you call out a category, all the children who can say Yes to that category stand up and change seats. Use your knowledge of the children to make sure that everyone has a go.

Closing Phase

Using 'Talking Ted', ask the children what they like about their families, e.g. parents to look after them, cook their meals, take them out, buy them toys, siblings to play with, pets to look after, etc.

"I like my family because _____ ."

Further Activities

Provide each child with a simple cut-out of a house. The children can stick photographs or draw family members on their house. Either the children or an adult writes on the names of the family. On the roof the children can write whose house it is, e.g. Sacha's House. The houses can be mounted as a wall display.

Whizz Chug Whirr

Learning Objectives

To find out about and identify the uses of everyday technology in the home.

Resources

Photographs or other illustrations of machines used in the home, e.g. vacuum cleaner, dishwasher, washing machine, food processor, sewing machine, telephone, computer.

Introductory Phase

Show the visual aids to the children. Ask them if they can tell you what each machine is called and what it does. Explain to the children that machines are made to help us.

Middle Phase

Using an example of one machine e.g. washing machine explain to the children how Mummies in the past had to spend all day washing clothes by hand.

Using miming actions, say the poem:

> Washing day, oh washing day, all I do is scrub.
> Mummy's, Daddy's, children's clothes, rub, rub, rub.
> Rinse them out, wring them out, peg them on the line.
> Oh dear! there's grey clouds in the sky, I hope it will stay fine.

Repeat this with the children copying the actions. Then say and mime actions to the following poem:

> Now I have a washing machine and it's so easy – look.
> I put the clothes in, press the switch, then read my favourite book!

Repeat this again as before.

Closing Phase

Put the children into two rows facing each other. Tell them that they are parts of a car washing machine. Let each child 'go through' the machine pretending to be a car, while the other children gently wash them. Ask the children for ideas of machines they'd like to help them - a machine for tidying their room, a machine to help them get dressed etc.

Further Activities

Using cardboard boxes, tubes and other art materials the children can make a machine. Ask the children to decide what the function of the machine is and what each part does. This activity can be done in small groups if you prefer.

In groups of four or five the children mime a machine working. Each child is a different part of the machine and performs a different action. Talk through with the children what the machine does and what each component part is for. The children can also make machine noises.

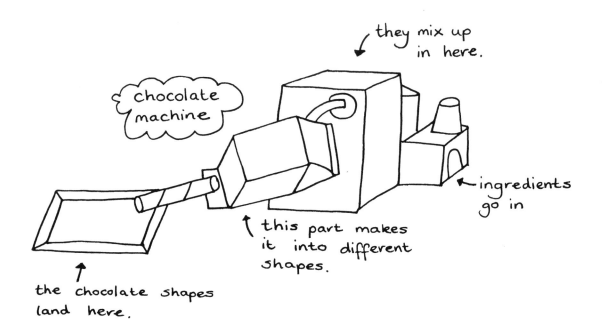

People from Near and Far

Learning Objectives

To look at and learn about different ethnic groups.

Resources

Photographs of people from different ethnic groups, some in different costume, e.g. Eskimo, African, Indian, Chinese. A small selection of foreign bric-a-brac; if you ask around, most parents, other staff or friends have some foreign souvenirs. A suitable age-related book about the life of a child in a foreign country, e.g. Dorling Kindersley's 'A Child like Me.'

Introductory Phase

Ask the children if they all look the same. What are the differences in hair colour, skin colour, height etc? Let the children look at the visual aids. Tell them that the people shown all come from different countries. Discuss with the children how the people look. Ask the children if they can think of any other ways in which the people differ, e.g. the food they eat, the types of houses they live in or the language they speak. Ask if any of the children have been to another country. What was it like?

Middle Phase

Show and discuss with the children the souvenirs that you have brought in. Encourage them to make comments and initiate discussion.

Closing Phase

Read the story that you have chosen about the child from another country.

Further Activities

Develop an art activity such as mask-making or a shell picture from an item of bric-a-brac.

Look at the life of a child from another country in more detail. Encourage the children to make comments on what is different and what is the same as in their own lives.

Around the World

Learning Objectives

To find out about and identify features of different geographical locations.

Resources

Three or four large illustrations of different geographical locations, e.g. jungle, desert, wide plains, mountain area, arctic region.

Introductory Phase

Look at the illustrations with the children. Ask them to comment on what they can see. Do they have such an area near to where they live? Do they know what such an area is called? Encourage the children to think about and offer suggestions as to what each area might be like, e.g. the temperature, rainfall, animals, buildings, people who might live there.

Middle Phase

Choose one of the locations. Tell the children they are going to pretend to be there and mime their actions. They can do this activity in the centre of the circle. Talk the children through what is happening. If the location is a jungle you might say:

> "It's very overgrown; push aside the creepers that are hanging down. You have to stoop down a bit to get under some of them. Now climb over a fallen tree trunk. Listen, what is that noise? Hissssss, I think it is a snake in the tree. Can you hear it? Hisssss. Look over there. I can see yellow and black stripes through the trees. It looks like a tiger. Be very quiet; walk on tip-toe. We don't want to disturb it."

If the location is a desert, you might say:

"You are walking on the sand. There is sand everywhere you look. It is hard to walk on the sand as your feet sink in. You have to pick up your feet very slowly and each time you take a step, you feel your feet sinking. The sun is very hot. It is making you feel very hot and tired. You are walking slower and slower. You would like a nice cool drink of water. You are so hot and tired that you have to crawl on your hands and knees, very slowly. At last you find a pool of water and you have a long drink."

The children can also offer suggestions.

Closing Phase

Look at the locations with the children again. Using 'Talking Ted', end with a round of:

"The place I like best is _____ because _____ ."

Further Activities

Turn the classroom into a jungle, making hanging creepers, big leaves and bright flowers, cut-out models of animals and birds.

Make a mountain range from a chicken wire and scrunched up newspaper base covered in DIY filler.

Town and Country

Learning Objectives

To learn about different environments and talk about features they like/dislike.

Resources

Some books and illustrations of town and countryside. The story of the town mouse and the country mouse, 'Tilly and Milly' by Katey Summers published by Orion.

Introductory Phase

Ask the children if they live in the town or the countryside. Let them spend some time looking at the books and illustrations. Ask what sorts of thing they might see in a town, e.g. houses, shops, library, cinema, factory, and what they might see in the countryside, e.g. houses, barns, woods, fields, lakes. Discuss with the children the types of animal they might see in either location. Ask them what they think are the good and bad things about living in either location.

Middle Phase

Read the story of the town mouse and the country mouse to show that there are different preferences.

Closing Phase

Using 'Talking Ted', end with a round of:

"I think I would like the town/country best because _____ ."

Further Activities

The children could make a collage of a town or the countryside using art materials and cut-out magazine illustrations or drawings.

Arrange a trip to a town centre and a countryside location then discuss with the children what they saw.

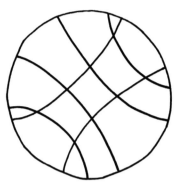

The Six Areas of Learning

5. Physical Development

'Young children's physical development is inseparable from all other aspects of development because they learn through being active and interactive' – QCA Curriculum Guidance

Learning objectives covered in this section are:

- Move with confidence, imagination and in safety

- Move with control and co-ordination

- Show awareness of space, of themselves and of others

- Recognise the importance of keeping healthy

- Recognise the changes that happen to their bodies when they are active

- Use a range of equipment

- Travel around, under, over and through equipment

Musical Movements

Learning Objectives

To move with confidence and imagination.

Resources

A cassette tape of different short musical excerpts and player.

Introductory Phase

Ask the children to watch and copy you as you perform a series of simple movements to the tempo of the music. Tell them to concentrate really hard on keeping in time to the beat.

Middle Phase

Choose a musical excerpt and decide beforehand what the music suggests to you, e.g. a circus, a storm, a hot summer's day. Discuss with the children the sorts of thing they might do in that situation. Play the excerpt again and let the children mime activities to the music. If there is sufficient time repeat the exercise with a contrasting piece of music.

Closing Phase

Tell the children to sit with their eyes closed and listen carefully as you play a different piece of music. Tell the children to consider, while the music is playing, what it makes them think of. When the excerpt has finished ask the children for their thoughts.

Using ' Talking Ted', end with a round of:

"The music made me think of _____ ."

Further Activities

Work out a short exercise or dance routine to music with the children.

Play any favourite pieces of music the children bring in.

Pirates and giants

Learning Objectives

To move with control and co-ordination, move with confidence and imagination.

Resources

Ball, plastic hoop, something to represent the giant's dinner, blindfold.

Introductory Phase

Tell the children that they must watch you carefully and copy your movements. Clap twice and touch a body part such as the head with both hands. Continue in this manner:

Clap, clap touch ears
Clap, clap touch knees
Clap, clap touch shoulders
Clap, clap touch feet.

As the children become more proficient, speed up the actions.

Middle Phase

Game of The Pirate's Treasure. Place the ball (the pirate's treasure) on an island (inside the hoop) in the centre of the circle. Choose a 'pirate' to guard the treasure. The children move into the circle and try to capture the treasure. If the pirate tags a child she must return to her seat. If a child succeeds in capturing the treasure he becomes the new pirate.

Closing Phase

Game of The Giant's Dinner. A 'giant' sits on a chair in the centre of the circle wearing a blindfold. In front of him is his 'dinner'. One at a time, children creep into the circle to try and steal the giant's dinner. If the giant hears them he shouts,

"I hear someone in my castle"

... and points in the direction of the sound. If the giant is correct, the intruder returns to her seat and another child has a go. Obviously, the children must stay very quiet during this game.

Further Activities

Another similar game is the giant's garden. A 'giant' is chosen to guard a garden in the centre of the circle. Card flowers are placed on the floor near the giant. In groups of four or five the children enter the circle and try to capture a flower. Any child tagged by the giant must return to his seat at once.

The children can role-play being giants or pirates, making an appropriate set from equipment in the nursery, i.e. a giant's castle or a pirate's ship.

The children could paint a picture of the giant's garden.

Slow and Fast

Learning Objectives

To move with control and co-ordination, show awareness of space, of themselves and of others.

Resources

None.

Introductory Phase

The children stand in a circle and then crouch down on hands and knees. They must crawl slowly forward until they reach the other side of the circle. The object of the game is that they must not touch anyone else so must take avoidance action if anyone gets in their way. Any child who bumps into another is out.

Middle Phase

The children walk quickly in a clockwise direction pretending to be cars. They may overtake other cars, but not change direction. At the signal 'red light' all cars must stop and look at you. Any cars that fail to do so or who bump into other cars must go into the garage for repairs and miss a turn.

Closing Phase

Using 'Talking Ted', end with a round of:

"I liked going fast/slow best because _____ ."

Further Activities

In a large outdoor space, make up a more complex traffic system for the children to pretend to be cars on. Include areas where they must halt, two way and one way roads, roundabouts etc.

Have a snail race to see who can move the slowest without actually stopping.

Have other animal races e.g. kangaroo-jumping, bunny-hopping.

Ball Games

Learning Objectives

To use equipment, show awareness of space, of themselves and of others.

Resources

Large and small balls, balloons.

Introductory Phase

The children sit on the floor with legs apart. Stand in the centre and roll the large ball to each child in turn. Call the child's name as you roll the ball. The child then rolls the ball back to you.

Middle Phase

The children stand in a circle and pass the ball round, first in a clockwise then in an anti-clockwise direction. Stand in the centre and throw the ball/balloon randomly to the children, calling the child's name first.

Using a small ball for older children and a large ball for younger children, the children roll the ball across the circle trying to make it leave the circle through any spaces. The other children try to keep the ball in the circle, using their legs and hands.

Closing Phase

Using the ball as the 'talking object', end with a round of:

"If I was a ball, I could bounce as high as _____ ."

Further Activities

The children can work singly or in pairs trying to bounce and catch a ball.

Play skittles with the children. The children could make their own set of skittles from empty plastic bottles.

Stepping Stones

Learning Objectives

To move with control and co-ordination, use a range of equipment, travel over balancing and climbing equipment.

Resources

Low-level climbing equipment, e.g. blocks, benches, pile of mats, bean bag seats, arranged in a continuous circle. Make sure that there is adequate adult supervision.

Introductory Phase

The children follow each other round the circle using
the apparatus to climb and walk on. They must try not to step on the floor.

Middle Phase

Ask the children if they can think of other ways of moving along the apparatus,
e.g. crawling, bottom shuffling. Let them try out different ways under adult
supervision.

Closing Phase

Ask the children if anyone would like to show the others their different ways of
moving. The other children sit around the circle and watch. After each child has
demonstrated say:

"Well done _____ ."

Further Activities

Build up skills and confidence on other climbing apparatus.

Let the children in groups of five or six make their own obstacle courses using
low-level climbing apparatus, tunnels etc.

Animal Antics

Learning Objectives

To move with imagination, control and co-ordination, show awareness of space, of themselves and of others.

Resources

None, but make sure that the children have enough space to do the activities.

Introductory Phase

Tell the children that they are going to play some animal games. First, they are going to pretend to be different animals and move like each animal, for example:

Bears	Walking on all fours, keeping limbs straight
Frogs	Jumping in a crouched position, using hands and feet
Kangaroos	Jumping in an upright position
Worms	Lying down and wriggling forwards
Birds	Flapping arms

Middle Phase

Game of Fishes in the Sea. The children stand in an inward-facing circle and are named 'cod', 'haddock' or 'plaice' (just use two names with young children). When the name of a fish is called out, all the children with that name move in a clockwise direction around the outside of the circle and back to their places. They are instructed how to move by various commands. Use as many different commands as you think the children will remember:

High tide	Walk quickly
Low tide	Walk slowly
Tide turns	Change direction
Fishermen about	Crawl on hands and knees to avoid nets
Sharks	Walk backwards
Rocks ahead	Jump

Closing phase

End with a round of:

"If I were an animal I would be _____ ."

Further Activities

The children could make up a 'zoo' in which pairs of children pretend to be different animals. Discuss each animal's environment, what they would eat, what they would do etc.

Make a fishing game using cut out card fish shapes which the children colour in. On the front of each fish attach a metal paper clip then make a fishing line from a wooden spill, cotton and magnet.

Fidgety Feet

Learning Objectives

To move with control and co-ordination, show awareness of space, of themselves and of others.

Resources

None. The children work barefoot. Make sure that they have sufficient space to do the activities.

Introductory Phase

Tell the children that today they are going to do some activities with their feet. Ask the children to look at their feet. What are they like? What do they use them for?

Middle Phase

Ask the children to see if they can stand on tip-toe. Up then down again. Repeat this several times. Can they balance on one foot – then the other. Repeat. Stand with feet together – jump and land with feet apart. Repeat several times. March on the spot – count time for them.

Closing Phase

Tell the children that they are going to pretend to walk around the circle on different surfaces. Mime the actions for them to copy.

Walking on squelchy mud	Feet are stuck and have to be pulled out at each step
Walking on a hot pavement	On tip-toe, lifting each foot as quickly as possible
On sand	Wriggle toes in sand
On a balancing beam	One foot in front of the other, arms out to keep balance
On a plank	Step sideways and move one foot up to the other

Close the activities by asking the children to sit on the floor with their legs stretched out in front of them. Together, they say:

"Well done feet for working hard! Now you can have a rest."

Further Activities

Make feet prints and display them on the wall. Label
each one _____'s foot; (you can depict wet sand when foot painting by mixing
sand with yellow paint).

Draw around the feet, cut out the shapes and make pictures with them, e.g. a
flower with 'feet' petals, a bird with 'feet' wings.

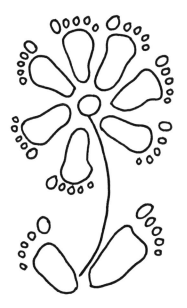

Parachute Games 1

Learning Objectives

To move with confidence, control and co-ordination, show awareness of space, of themselves and of others, use equipment.

Resources

A suitably sized parachute for the group you are working with; (it may be possible to borrow a parachute from your local Under Five's Resource Centre or buy one from the Positive Press catalogue.)

Introductory Phase

Make sure that you have sufficient adult helpers to control the parachute.

The children stand around the parachute, holding it at waist height. On the count of three, they raise their arms to make the parachute mushroom and shout hello at the opposite player.

Middle Phase

Game of Deliver a Parcel. The children stand around the parachute, holding it at waist height. A small, light box is placed in the centre and all the children work together to ripple or tilt the parachute so that the box is moved to a named child.

Game of Make a Tent. The children crouch down around the parachute, holding it with both hands. On the count of three, they raise their arms to make the parachute mushroom, step forward under it, then pull it down behind them and sit on the edge of it. Someone can stand in the centre to be the tent pole.

Closing Phase

Game of Row the Boat. The children sit cross-legged
around the parachute, holding it with both hands. Tell the children that they are
going to pretend that the parachute is a special round boat that has been made
just for them They all make gentle rowing movements and sing:

> Row, row, row the boat, gently down the stream
> Merrily, merrily, merrily, merrily, life is but a dream.

Tell the children to imagine that they are getting out of the boat to lay down on
the grass and close their eyes and rest.

Further Activities

See end of Parachute Games 2.

Parachute Games 2

Learning Objectives

To move with confidence, control and co-ordination, show awareness of space, of themselves and of others, use equipment.

Resources

See Parachute Games 1.

Introductory Phase

Greetings Game. The children stand around the parachute, holding it at waist height. Two children from opposite sides are chosen to perform a greeting ritual e.g. hug, shake hands. On the count of three the children raise their arms to make the parachute mushroom. The two children run under the parachute and greet one another, then go back to their places. Repeat with two different players until all the children have had a go.

Middle Phase

Changing Places Game. The children stand around the parachute, holding it at waist height. Call out different categories, e.g. anyone with black hair, anyone whose name begins with J. Decide with the children before they carry out the action who fits into the category you have called. On the count of three, the children make the parachute mushroom and those children in the named category run underneath and change places.

Game of Storm at Sea. A few children at a time lie on top of the parachute, in the centre. They pretend they are in a small boat at sea. The other children sit around the outside, holding the parachute in both hands. Tell them to make gentle sea waves then talk them through a storm, increasing the wave movements. Gradually reduce the wave movements after the storm until the sea is calm again.

Closing Phase

Game of Underground Tunnels. The children sit or crouch around the parachute, which is on the ground. One or more players are chosen to name a child on the other side of the circle. The children then crawl under the parachute and tunnel in the direction of the named child. The other children gently ripple the parachute.

To close the activities, ask the children to sit quietly by the parachute with hands in laps. Tell them to breathe in (to the count of five) then out (to the count of five). Do this several times.

Further Activities

Try different objects on top of the parachute to see if they move differently, e.g. a ball, a feather, a flat tray.

The children could make flat card boats to sail across the parachute sea.

Make card cut-outs of parachutes. Ask the children to bring in a photograph of themselves that can be cut up. Let the children each paint a parachute in bright colours, then cut out the figures of the children from the photographs and attach them to their parachutes with cotton. Make a wall display with a blue sky background and a few white clouds and attach the parachutes.

Keeping Fit

Learning Objectives

To recognise the importance of keeping healthy, to recognise changes that happen to their bodies when they are active.

Resources

None, but make sure that the circle is big enough to do the activities.

Introductory Phase

Send various actions around the circle, e.g. wiggle fingers, tap knees, touch toes to warm up the children.

Middle Phase

Stand in the centre of the circle and do some simple keep fit exercises for the children to copy, e.g. stretching, bending, swinging arms, jumping.

Closing Phase

Ask the children to tell you how they feel when they exercise - hot, out of breath, sweaty. Depending on the age and understanding of the children, you can talk to them about their hearts beating faster and how sweat is produced to cool them down. Discuss with the children how exercise makes heart and muscles stronger and this is good for keeping healthy. A good way to calm down after exercise is to mime being a melting snowman. Do this with the children, explaining that they must slowly and gradually become smaller until they are a 'puddle on the floor'.

Further Activities

Divide the children into groups of four or five and let them devise their own exercise routine.

The children could do a project on health looking at exercise, food etc.

The Six Areas of Learning

6. Creative Development

'Children's creativity develops most productively within a rich learning environment supported by interventions of sensitive and responsive adults'
– QCA Curriculum Guidance

Learning objectives covered in this section are :

◆ Explore colour, texture, shape in two and three dimensions

◆ Recognise and explore how sounds can be changed, sing simple songs from memory, recognise repeated sounds and sound patterns and match movements to music

◆ Respond in a variety of ways to what they see, hear and feel

◆ Use their imagination in art and design, music, dance, imaginative and role play and stories

◆ Express and communicate their ideas, thoughts and feelings by using a widening range of materials, imaginative and role play, movement, designing and making and a variety of songs and musical instruments

The Feely Game

Learning Objectives

To explore texture and shape.

Resources

Collect enough objects for one per child which have interesting textures and shapes and are safe to handle, e.g. a sponge, a hairbrush, a smooth pebble, a bean bag etc. Put all the objects into a bag. A blindfold.

Introductory Phase

Invite each child in turn to put on the blindfold and take an object from the bag. Warn the other children in advance not to call out what the object is. Ask the child to describe what the object feels like. Encourage the children to use a variety of words like hard, lumpy, prickly, smooth, knobbly, soft, squishy. When the child has described the object, invite the other children to volunteer more words. The children take their objects back to their seats.

Middle Phase

Ask the children to look at and describe the shape of their object. Again encourage the children to use as many different words as they can, such as long, short, fat, thin, round, square, twisty, pointy, curly.

Closing Phase

Ask the children to put the objects into different categories like hard/soft, rough/smooth. Suggest two and then invite the children to think of some more different ones. You could place two different coloured boxes or carpet squares on the floor to help younger children.

Further Activities

Make up a display board of small squares of differently textured materials, e.g. cloths, sandpaper, rubber etc.

Give the children a 'shape' of play-dough and work with them on making different shapes from it.

Collect natural items like leaves and fruits and look at all the different shapes.

The Magic Cloak

Learning Objectives

To use imagination in role play and communicate ideas.

Resources

Cloak. Cauldron or box to represent cauldron. Wooden spoon or stick.

Introductory Phase

Introduce the 'magic cloak' to the children and tell them that they are going to pretend that anyone who wears the cloak can do magic. In the first game, the 'magician' can turn the other children into anything he chooses, for example:

> "I turn you into babies, giants, tigers, worms etc"

The other children perform a suitable action until you call 'Stop'. Then a different magician is chosen.

Middle Phase

Game of Making Spells. For this game you need a magician and an apprentice. The magician thinks of a good spell, e.g. the sun will shine, a cheering-up spell. The children volunteer appropriate ingredients to go into the cauldron. Encourage the children to think of different things for each spell and to make them related. To make the sun shine they might use yellow flowers, hot coals, oranges etc. A cheering-up spell could require a joke book, a cuddly toy, some sweets etc. The apprentice mimes collecting the ingredients from the children and putting them into the cauldron. The magician stirs the ingredients together with the wooden spoon, while everyone chants:

> "Stir them round and stir them thick,
> our magic spell will do the trick."

The magician sprinkles the spell over the other children and they mime a suitable response, pretending the sun is shining, pretending to be cheerful.

Closing Phase

The wearer of the cloak can transform himself into any animal, miming appropriate actions and making relevant sounds such as a cat on all fours saying miaow. The other children have to guess the animal. The child who guesses correctly then becomes the magician. Younger children may need some whispered prompting to suggest what to mime. To end the activities, you become the magician and tell the children that you are going to turn them into sleeping lions. They must all lie down, close their eyes and pretend to sleep.

Further Activities

The children can make cloaks from crepe paper and glue on tin foil stars and moons.

Talk to the children about ingredients in cooking and make up a batch of gingerbread dough. Let the children use star and moon dough cutters, then cook the biscuits for them to take home.

Dream Bedrooms

Learning Objectives

To use imagination in art and design.

Resources

None.

Introductory Phase

Talk to the children about their bedrooms. Ask them for details, e.g. do they have cabin beds, bunks? What designs are on their curtains, duvet covers? What furniture is in their rooms? What do they like about their rooms?

Ask the children what would they have if they could choose their dream bedrooms. Encourage fantasy, e.g. a bed made of chocolate, a bed like Captain Hook's pirate ship, a jungle painted on the walls, a round soft bed like a marshmallow. Talk about colours they would like and accessories.

Middle Phase

Play a game of 'sleeping dogs'. The children lie down and pretend to be asleep. You can tell jokes or say things to make them laugh and move. Any child who moves is out. The last child left 'asleep' is the winner.

Closing Phase

Divide the children into small groups of four or five with an adult supervisor for each group. Discuss with the children the bedroom they will make and what will go in it.

End with a round of

"In my bedroom, I would like _____ ."

Further Activities

Allow the children to construct a model of a bedroom in a large cardboard box with the front cut away. They can do this in small groups, pairs or individually depending on the level of adult help that you have. They can construct simple furniture from boxes and cartons and cut-out illustrations from magazines. Ask the children to think carefully about what they would need in a bedroom.

Talk to the children about the purpose of each room in a house and what is needed in a particular room – kitchen, dining room, bathroom, lounge and so on.

Dance Steps

Learning Objectives

To match movements to music, use imagination in dance.

Resources

A cassette tape of music suitable for the activities.

Introductory Phase

Use a set dance for this phase, either a country dance or one that you have made up. For example:

> Hold hands in a circle. Take six side steps to the right followed by six side steps to the left. Move into the centre of the circle, arms raised, back out again. Repeat. Hold hands crossed with a partner and circle on the spot then parade with partner around the circle.

Practise this routine with the children. You can simplify it for younger children by just using the first four movements or devise your own routine. When you feel that the children are ready, play a suitable piece of music for them to dance to.

Middle Phase

Creative dance: play a piece of music and ask the children to dance like giants, fairies, old people, string puppets, robots etc.

Closing Phase

Using 'Talking Ted', end with a round of:

> "The dancing I liked best was _____ because _____ ."

Further Activities

Allow the children to organise a disco where they can wear special clothes and bring in their own music to play and dance to.

Try and obtain a video of different types of dancing, e.g. ballet, flamenco, street, ballroom. Show this to the children and discuss it with them.

Arrange a dance 'show' performed by the children for other classes/parents.

Making Music

Learning Objectives

To explore and recognise sounds, respond to what they hear and touch, express ideas using musical instruments, explore how sounds can be changed.

Resources

A selection of percussion instruments such as triangle and beater, maracas, tambourine, castanets, cymbal, drum – enough for one per child. A large cardboard box placed on a table.

Introductory Phase

Introduce the instruments, telling the children the name of each one. Ask them to repeat the name after you (you can simplify the names if you wish, e.g. shaker for maracas). Put three or four of the instruments into the box on the table and, ensuring that the children can't see your movements, make a sound with one of the instruments. Ask the children to guess which one it was. Show the children the instrument then repeat this procedure with another instrument.

Middle Phase

Hand out the instruments so that each child has one. It may be easier to keep them in different sections, e.g. all tambourines in one part of the circle. In turn, play each different instrument. Ask the children what they think each one sounds like. Maracas could sound like rain, cereals in a box etc. Sing together a familiar song or nursery rhyme and ask the children to beat time with their instruments while you conduct – with older children you can add 'volume control', using your hands (palms inwards). As you move your hands apart the volume increases, as you bring your hands together the volume decreases. To turn the volume 'off' turn palms outwards towards the children.

Closing Phase

Collect in all the instruments except for one. Ask the children to see if they can pass it around the circle very carefully without it making a single sound.

Further Activities

Ask the helpers or parents if anyone plays an instrument that they could bring in and show/play to the children.

Set up a sound workshop day with the children divided into small groups. Each group can look at a different instrument sound, make instruments and/or experiment with producing different sounds. For strings:

Experiment with different thicknesses of rubber band and 'string' lengths to produce different sounds.

For Wind, use a set of similar bottles with different levels of water inside to produce sounds of varying pitch by blowing across the opening.

For Percussion, make drums with different skins e.g. leather, cloth, cling film, paper. Use chopsticks or spoons as beaters. Children also love to bang with spoons on a selection of kitchen utensils tied to a 'washing line'.

The children can make maracas by covering a slightly blown up balloon with papier maché. Leave to dry, remove balloon, paint and varnish. Fill with lentils, insert doweling and secure with tape.

Song Time

Learning Objectives

To recognise and explore how sounds can be changed and sing simple songs from memory.

Resources

None.

Introductory Phase

Tell the children that they have to watch very carefully as they will have to copy the sounds that you make. Sing different single notes in a variety of ways, e.g. high, low, soft, loud, short, long, with mouth wide open, with mouth nearly closed. Ask the children to repeat each note after you.

Middle Phase

Choose some familiar songs to sing together which are suitable for a circle, e.g. 'Ring o'roses', 'Here we go round the mulberry bush', 'In and out the dusty windows'.

Closing Phase

Choose a song with actions, e.g. 'My hat it has three corners'. Sing the song through with the accompanying actions. Then repeat several times leaving out additional words each time, but performing the appropriate actions.

My _____ it has three corners
My _____ it has _____ corners
My _____ it has _____ _____ etc.

To end on a calming note, sing the complete song again in a whisper.

Further Activities

Choose a familiar song which the children can dress up and mime actions to.

Use an occasion such as Easter or Christmas to make up a simple song with the children and sing it to a familiar tune.

Let the children take turns to choose a song that they like for everyone to sing together.

Picnic Time

Learning Objectives

To use imagination in role play, express and communicate ideas.

Resources

Two glove puppets.

Introductory Phase

Introduce the puppets to the children, e.g. Ritzy Rabbit, Hiccup Hedgehog, then continue with the following dialogue.

Ritzy Rabbit:	What a lovely day it is today Hiccup. The sun is shining, the sky is blue and there's not a cloud in sight.
Hiccup Hedgehog:	It's so nice Ritzy that we ought to do something special.
Ritzy Rabbit:	We could go out somewhere for a walk.
Hiccup Hedgehog:	That would be good, but I'd like to do something even more special.
Ritzy Rabbit:	I know Hiccup, let's have a picnic.
Hiccup Hedgehog:	Ooh yes, I love picnics, but what shall we take?
Ritzy Rabbit:	Let's ask the children to help us think of all the things we need to take.

Prompt the children to tell you the necessary items, e.g. chairs, rug, table cloth and what food you could include. The puppets can join in with comments like:

> "That's a good idea. I really like marmite sandwiches."

At the end of the discussion, the puppets thank the children for their help.

Middle Phase

Tell the children that they are going to pretend to have a picnic. Divide them into groups of four or five with an adult supervisor for each group. They prepare the food, drinks etc and place everything into an imaginary basket. The adult helper talks them through the mimes, for example:

> "Now let's make some sandwiches. We need two slices of bread then spread the butter on each slice. What will you put in your sandwich? I'm going to have ham in mine. Put the two slices together and cut them into four. Now we'll put our sandwich in a bag and put it in the picnic basket."

When the picnic is ready, decide with the children where they would like to have it, e.g. by the sea, in a wood, in a park. Pick up the picnic basket and tell the children to follow you as you walk to the 'picnic site'. There the children pretend to unpack the picnic basket and eat the food. Encourage the children to join in with comments and ask them questions like:

> "Is your sandwich delicious Sanjay?"
> "What would you like next Rosie?"

Finally, pick up all the litter and pack everything away.

Closing Phase

Bring the groups back to the circle. Using 'Talking Ted', end with a round of:

> "One thing I would take on my picnic is _____ ."

Further Activities

Arrange a real picnic for the children, even if it is an indoor event.

Let the children use puppets or bring in teddies to stage a picnic.

Make a wall display of a picnic. The children can draw or cut out magazine illustrations of the food.

Teach me a Song

Learning Objectives

To sing simple songs from memory.

Resources

A glove puppet.

Introductory Phase

Introduce the puppet to the children. Tell them that the puppet really likes to sing and would like them to teach him a song. Do the children know one that they could sing to him?

Middle Phase

Once you have agreed on a song, sing together while the puppet listens or 'dances' to the song. Let the puppet clap the children and say well done to them.

Closing Phase

The puppet tells the children that he is now going to teach them a new song. Would they like that? You can choose one from your own selection or use the one below, sung to the tune of 'Cock a doodle do, my dame has lost her shoe'.

> Cock a doodle do, my clock says half past two.
> I won't be back in time for lunch, whatever shall I do?

To end on a calm note, ask the children to close their eyes and think about their favourite lunch.

Further Activities

Arrange a singing session with a difference e.g. play a video of nursery rhymes that the children can watch and sing along to.

The children could have a karaoke session of singing to a cassette of nursery rhymes.

The Helping Genie

Learning Objectives

To use imagination, express and communicate ideas through role play.

Resources

None.

Introductory Phase

Tell the children that you are going to tell them a story about a genie. You want them to close their eyes and try and picture in their minds what is happening in the story. Now read out the story below.

Middle Phase

Imagine that you are a genie whose special job is to help people. One sunny day you are sitting in your garden looking at your beautiful flowers and listening to the birds sing.

A little boy comes into your garden and taps you on the arm. He looks very sad and you ask him what the matter is. The little boy tells you that he comes from a nearby village. It's a lovely village; the people are good and kind and everyone has always been very happy. However, now something dreadful has happened.

Every time the little boy and all the other children go out to play they hear a terrible rumble and the earth shakes. There are loud noises – clump, clump, clump – and then a big giant the size of a house appears over the hill. All the children are frightened that the giant wants to eat them and run indoors. Now they are too scared to go outside at all.

You tell the little boy that you will help him and decide to visit the giant in his castle.

It's a long way to the castle. The road is steep and winding. Think of yourself as you trudge slowly up this road. Your legs feel more tired and heavy with every step you take. But you are a genie with magical powers so you decide to turn yourself into a bird and fly instead.

At last you reach the castle gates. They are very big, think of them reaching up tall into the sky. You turn yourself back into a genie and creep through the gates.

Imagine how quietly you tip-toe through the castle. The rooms are huge, as big as a field and each step is as big as a table. Think of how you will manage to get up the steps.

You creep into the giant's parlour. On the table is the giant's breakfast. What does he have for breakfast. Think how much food he would eat.

Suddenly there is a loud clump, clump, clump. The giant is coming. You must use your magical powers to turn yourself into something so that the giant will not see you. What will you turn yourself into?

The giant strides into the room and sits down in his chair. There is a loud snuffling noise, then a splashing noise. You can't believe your eyes. The giant is crying great, big salty tears which run down his nose and plop with a splash onto the floor.

Now, you are a helping genie and you don't like to see anybody sad, even giants. You decide to speak to him and find out what is wrong, but how will you do this?

The giant tells you that he is lonely and has no friends. He has tried to make friends with the children in the village, but they just run away every time he appears. You explain to the giant why the children are afraid, but then tell the giant that they are kind children and if you talk to them they will not be afraid of him as long as he is gentle with them. The giant agrees and soon he is happily playing with the children and joining in their games.

You can adapt the story or talk it through as you read, for younger children.

Closing Phase

Ask the children to think of the games that the giant could play with the children. End with a round of:

"My favourite game is _____ ."

Further Activities

Let the children role-play the story. They could begin by pretending to be the village children, then take the role of the giant taking big strides etc. They could think of all sorts of helpful things the genie might do.

The children could work in small groups to paint a big picture of the giant.

A Strange Land

Learning Objectives

To use imagination, explore colour, to express ideas using a range of materials in art and design.

Resources

A variety of art materials, coloured paper, glue, scissors, cut-out magazine illustrations, paint. Part of this session will take place outside the circle.

Introductory Phase

Tell the children that they are going to think about visiting a strange and magical land where everything is different. They must close their eyes and try to picture in their heads what it looks like. Now read out the story below.

Middle Phase

First of all I will tell you about the trees and flowers. The trees are a funny colour; they have red, blue and purple trunks and all sorts of different coloured leaves. The flowers are different too and have strange shapes like spoons or curls. Some have spots or stripes of different colours.

There are birds in the trees; they are making very odd noises. Can you think what sorts of noise they might make? They do not look like the birds you see in your garden. What do you think they could look like?

Some little furry animals come up to you. They are not dogs or cats or rabbits. They are different from any of the animals that you know. What do you think they are like and what colour are they?

This is a very strange land. Even the sky, rivers and sea are different colours. Think about what colours they might be. Do you think you would like to live in this strange land?

Closing Phase

In groups of four or five and with as many helpers as possible, the children discuss and make a collage of a strange land. Encourage really fantastic ideas, e.g. a bird could be made up of a bird's body with a car front for a head and a bunch of flowers for a tail. The object of the exercise is to use imagination and have fun.

Further Activities

Talk to the children about 'strange lands' in stories like 'Alice in Wonderland'.

The children could role-play being strange birds and other animals, making funny noises.

Look in books for a few strange plants and animals that do exist and which would fascinate the children, e.g. insect-eating plants, a duck-billed platypus.

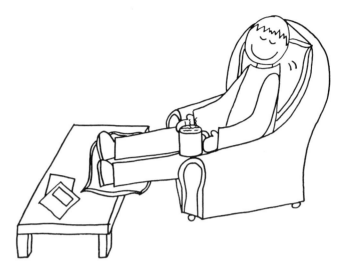

A last word...

Remember to consider your own energy levels!

Trying out new ideas and being creative, warm and positive all the time with young children can be exhausting.

You do need to look after yourself.

Have a 'Golden Moment' whenever you can – make a hot drink, put your feet up, relax with slow breathing, and reflect on all the positive things that have happened.

Training and Resources

Training Opportunities

Jenny Mosley Consultancies are able to offer a wide range of courses, all encompassed within the framework of her Whole School Quality Circle Time Model. We have a small team of highly experienced consultants available to meet the specific requirements of individual schools.

Courses we offer

Developing the Quality Circle Time Model: assessing and evaluating the effectiveness of your current policies for positive behaviour, creative lunchtimes and strategies for supporting teachers and children under stress.

Working with Children: a structured programme of practical Circle Time demonstrations with children, as well as evaluation with lunchtime supervisors and an action plan for a way forward – all within a 'normal school' day (i.e. not a closure day).

Other courses include:

Early Years and Quality Circle Time
Building self-esteem – parents and schools together
Building self-esteem with children
Effective communication with parents and children
Developing emotional intelligence for children
Developing all aspects of creative groupwork
Circle Time, citizenship and PSHE
Switching children on to learning
Drama and creative arts
Raising energy and morale of staff
Coping creatively with conflict
Achieving excellence through valuing individuals
Developing counselling skills

Accredited, specialist trainers only!

Our research and experience have revealed that the Whole School Quality Circle Time Model can become diluted or vulnerable when people who have never attended one of our in-depth courses themselves give training based on our model. Jenny Mosley holds five-day accredited 'Train the Trainers' courses nationally and then awards accompanying certificates.

**For details of all the above, contact the Project Manager
by any of the means listed on page 141.**

Books and other resources

Turn Your School Round by Jenny Mosley (LDA)

Best-selling management manual giving a clear picture of the Quality Circle Time approach, emphasising the need for it to be a whole school policy and including guidelines and practical examples for a range of situations.

Quality Circle Time in the Primary Classroom by Jenny Mosley (LDA)

Invaluable guide to getting started and building strategies to promote self-esteem and positive behaviour, for teachers wishing to put the Whole School Quality Circle Time model into their classrooms, with hundreds of ideas and lesson plans.

More Quality Circle Time by Jenny Mosley (LDA)

Sequel to the above enabling you to evaluate and enhance your current Circle Time practice, raising it to even more exciting and creative levels. Includes ten-minute circle times for nursery children to practise specific skills.

Photocopiable Materials for use with the Jenny Mosley Circle Time Model by Jenny Mosley (Positive Press)

Make life easier with a wealth of charts, target sheets, achievement ladders, awards, congratulations cards, invitations and much more, including tips to help you quickly put them to good use.

All Round Success by Jenny Mosley (Wiltshire County Council)

Simply set-out practical ideas and games for circle time, tried and tested in a year-long project with primary teachers.

Coming Round Again by Jenny Mosley (Wiltshire County Council)

Follows on from the above, pulling together a range of fun activities that provide excellent learning opportunities for PSHE and citizenship themes. Explains the rationale behind Circle Time and includes problem-solving ideas.

Circle Time (Positive Press)

User-friendly booklet built around Jenny Mosley's whole school approach, with practical lesson plans for KS1 and KS2 based on an original project in Belfast and now updated.

The Circle Book by Jenny Mosley (Positive Press)

A booklet of feedback and comments (by children and adults) originally compiled in response to the Elton Report (1989) and building on research study results. Updated with more ideas for activities.

Working Towards a Whole School Policy on Self-Esteem and Positive Behaviour by Jenny Mosley (Positive Press)

A booklet of guidelines for operating an effective policy involving teachers, MDSAs, parents, governors and children.

Guidelines for Primary Midday Supervisors by Jenny Mosley (Wiltshire County Council)

A friendly self-help booklet for lunchtime supervisors to use in developing skills in their role as positive models for the children, supporting your school in the creation of secure and happy playtimes.

Create Happier Lunchtimes by Jenny Mosley (Wiltshire County Council)

Sequel to the above, reminding lunchtime supervisors of the importance of their role, offering extra ideas and both indoor and outdoor games.

Assemblies to Teach Golden Rules by Margaret Goldthorpe and Lucy Nutt (LDA)

Ideal if your assemblies could use more 'pep'! Scripts and ideas for creative, fun presentations themed on the moral values behind Golden Rules, based on positive reward for good behaviour rather than punishment for negative actions.

Poems for Circle Time and Literacy Hour by Margaret Goldthorpe (LDA)

A much loved book by one of Jenny's senior consultants. Poems of simplicity and fun introduce children in a relaxed way to serious issues such as bullying and can then provide the theme for circle time.

Training video: Quality Circle Time in Action (LDA)

Introduced and performed by Jenny Mosley and ideal for staff training, this video demonstrates the model in use with unrehearsed KS1 and KS2 children. The phases and their rationale are explained by Jenny using many of the resources listed here for sale. With accompanying handbook.

Jenny Mosley's Self-Esteem Builders Kit

Set of colourful high-quality resources to get your school quickly started with Quality Circle Time. Contains motivational stickers for congratulating children on moral values and circle time skills; two colourful themed class target sheets with reusable stickers to mark progress in positive behaviour; reward certificates for achievements such as deciding to improve; responsibility badges for boosting children's self-esteem through special tasks; and a golden rules poster set for classroom and playground. Items also available separately.

Jenny Mosley's Quality Circle Time Kitbag

Costume and treasures to inspire creative circle times: contains 'magic' cloak, blindfold, hand-painted egg (for use as talking object), South American rainstick, small teddy bear, two charming hand puppets and 'treasure chest', together with cassette tape and booklet of lesson ideas. Rainstick, eggs and puppets also available separately.

Playground Friends Baseball Cap

Brightly coloured incentive to support your whole school lunchtime policy, which advocates choosing pupil helpers to befriend marginalised or bewildered children. A 'badge of office' to be worn with pride. Playground Stops for children seeking help also in preparation.

Golden Moments Mug

In eye-catching blue and gold, for your very own use when you stop and enjoy a moment of relaxation after the creative demands of circle time.

Further titles and products in preparation from Positive Press:

Resources: Parachutes for circle time

Books: All Year Round – a book of happier lunchtimes
                              Golden Moments for Busy Teachers

We also have books on Quality Circle Time for transition and secondary schools, and on self-esteem and assertiveness for adults ... ask for details.

For further details and to order contact:
Jenny Mosley Consultancies / Positive Press Ltd
Tel. 01225 767157   Fax. 01225 755631
E-mail circletime@jennymosley.demon.co.uk

28A Gloucester Road
Trowbridge
Wiltshire
BA14 0AA

Website www.circle-time.co.uk